Beverley Call...

THE COMPLETE REAL RESULTS BOOK

A COMPREHENSIVE GUIDE TO A HEALTHY AND MORE ACTIVE LIFE STYLE

CHAMELEON

First published in Great Britain in 1997 by
Chameleon Books
106 Great Russell Street
London WC1B 3LJ

© 1997 Chameleon Books

A catalogue record for this book is available from the British Library.

Contributors: Jane Bartlett, Darryl Preston B.Ed.P.E. and Sybil Greatbatch

ISBN 0 233 990607

Printed and bound in Italy by Editoriale Bortolazzi Stei

Contents

For Rebecca and Joshua

WITH SPECIAL THANKS TO:
Jane Fonda for inspiration, Steven, Jacky, Jane, Darryl,
Jim Carter, John Cuppello, everyone who comes to my classes and
the team who helped and supported me throughout this project.

Hello

Welcome to my Real Results exercise and healthy eating book. I'm Beverley Callard, and I've brought out this book because I think that exercise can make a real difference to everyone's life. It certainly has to mine.

I've been a fitness enthusiast for years, long before I first appeared in *Coronation Street*. I exercise because I love it; it improves my life in so many ways, because I feel good from the inside out. Exercise helps you achieve the body shape you want, makes you sizzle with good health and energy - and it's great fun. If you think exercise is boring, you've been doing the wrong kind of routine.

I was always keen on sports at school, especially swimming and netball, but got serious about exercise following a car crash in 1978. I smashed my left leg badly and needed physiotherapy for months. The more exercise I did, the better my leg healed. That was the start of it. Then the Jane Fonda boom hit the country. Everybody was setting up aerobics classes in church halls, so I went to a class run by one of my friends. I ended up going five nights a week, it was such good fun. Then my friend asked me if I'd like to have a go at teaching. I took myself off on various courses to try and learn more about it. Then I headed classes myself, combining it with my acting career.

Teaching exercise is one of the great joys of my life. The only time I stopped taking classes was during my first 18 months in *Coronation Street*, when my son Josh was just a baby. I really missed it; I was low in energy, felt easily stressed and suffered with insomnia. Then one day, when watching myself on television, I realised I was getting fat. I knew I had to do something about it, so I joined a gym.

I limit my class to 25 people to keep it personal and safe. They're all normal people, with busy lives, families and homes to run. Exercising can even be a family affair; I have a mother and daughter who attend, and sometimes my daughter Rebecca makes a class. My pupils range in age from 16 to 62 and are of all abilities. You'll meet some of the girls in the book, telling their own stories about how exercising has helped shape them. You'll meet my mum too! She's 66 and for the past four years has been working out every morning, proving that it's never too late to start.

Sadly, not everyone can join my class in Bolton, where I could show you in person the Real Results that exercise can bring about in your life. So I've brought out this book, written in consultation with the UK's leading fitness instructor Darryl Preston - B.Ed.P.E., the author and health journalist Jane Bartlett, and nutritionist Sybil Greatbatch. This isn't a book which promises the unrealistic. All the advice is sensible and proven; no fads, no gimmicks. But the results can at times seem magical. One of the biggest thrills I get

as a fitness teacher is watching people in my class improve their body shape. They literally chisel themselves out a new, well-toned slim figure, and find a new confidence and self-esteem.

In Body Matters we take a voyage around your body, where you'll learn some essential biology about the human machine. We look at how and why exercise makes you super healthy, both in body and mind. Then it's down to work with my exercise routine. I've also included six exercises for your face. Like any other part of the body, it has muscles which can go droopy with age. Just ten minutes of facial exercises every day can help delay the signs of ageing and give you a youthful glow.

In Shape Up Your Life you'll get crucial advice about optimum nutrition and speedy but safe slimming. There are delicious recipes specially designed for those with little time to spare. Finally we cool down with a guide to stress-proofing your life. If you're anything like me, your life is busy and stressful; learning how to relax is vital.

I want this book to be your friend, something that really supports you and is at your side every step of the way. I've included a yearly workout plan to guide you through the months ahead. You can use it to chart your progress.

One of the hardest things about exercise is actually starting and making it part of your life. You've made a positive step by buying this book, so don't waste your money - go for it, use it. Exercise and healthy living has had Real Results for me, and I know it can work for you too.

Good luck!

Body Matters

Imagine how it would feel if you suddenly found yourself in a gorgeous, lean and well-toned body. Being in that body makes you feel strong, supple and sexy. You find it easy to perform all the tasks of daily life. You go out and buy yourself a new wardrobe of fashionable, figure hugging clothes. You are happier and far less anxious, brimming with energy. At work you are more alert and haven't had a day off sick for ages. You sleep well and wake up refreshed.

You might say that it would take a miracle to bring about such positive changes in your life. All it could actually take is something very ordinary and available to all: physical exercise. The benefits of having a fit body can be pretty miraculous. You will find that exercise not only shapes you physically, it shapes your entire life.

SO WHAT DOES IT TAKE TO BE FIT?
YOU WILL NEED TO DEVELOP THE THREE 'S's:
Suppleness, Strength and Stamina

Suppleness

This means being able to stretch your body; bend, reach out and twist. If you are supple, you are less likely to pull your muscles and get stiff. Muscles which are not stretched regularly will shorten, limiting the movement in your joints. Stretching exercises are great if you want to become flexible.

Strength

This means you are able to exert force for pushing, pulling and lifting. Being strong will help you with all sorts of everyday activities, like carrying heavy bags of shopping home, lifting children, digging the garden and even opening up stubborn jars. A strong back and tummy will help you maintain a good posture. Exercises like press-ups or weight training help improve your strength.

Stamina

This is the ability to keep on going. You need stamina if you are going to be able to walk up a hill or run for a bus without collapsing in a heap, gasping for breath. Aerobic exercise is the best way to improve stamina. It's called aerobic because it makes you breath in more oxygen for your working muscles.

HOW MUCH EXERCISE DO YOU NEED TO DO EACH WEEK TO STAY FIT?

a) Three sessions of vigorous aerobic exercise lasting 20 minutes.

b) Five sessions of moderate activity lasting 30 minutes.

Answer: Either. Until recently it was recommended that each week you should have at least three sessions of vigorous aerobic exercise lasting 20 minutes or more. These recommendations are still valid, although in 1994 a complementary set of guidelines was added. New research indicated the benefits of more frequent, but moderate exercise - good news for those who loathe building up a sweat. The new recommendation is that you have at least five sessions each week of 30 minutes moderate activity.

VIGOROUS ACTIVITY:

Sports and exercises such as squash, running, football, swimming, tennis, aerobics and cycling, at a level of effort which makes you sweat and leaves you out of breath.

MODERATE ACTIVITY:

Long walks at a brisk or fast pace (at least 4 mph); heavy housework (spring cleaning); heavy gardening. Sports and exercise undertaken at a level which does not make you sweat or leave you out of breath.

Make friends with your body

You don't have to be a professor of anatomy, but if you want to get fit it helps if you know the basics of the highly engineered human body. Being aware of what is going on in your body on a day to day basis gives you a good insight into why we all need some level of exercise. Cars left standing on the roadside soon seize up with rust, their batteries are left to go flat; so it is with your body. It's also helpful to have some perception of what is happening inside that human machine as you put it through its paces. You could visualise your heart pumping efficiently and your muscles increasing in strength and definition. Insight into your body's workings will help you stay motivated.

Bev says...

If you have a bit of knowledge about your biology it can help you focus when you exercise. You will know what muscle groups you are working at any given time. For instance, each time you lift your shoulders away from the floor during the abdominal crunch you can imagine that abominal muscle going right down the centre of the abdomen, contracting and expanding. If you focus you'll see improvements sooner.

HOW MUCH DO YOU KNOW ABOUT YOUR BODY?

GIVE YOUR BRAIN A WORK-OUT WITH THIS QUICK BIOLOGY QUIZ.

1. HOW MANY MUSCLES ARE THERE IN THE BODY?
   a) 620
   b) 170
   c) 1,822

2. WHAT SIZE IS AN AVERAGE HEART?
   a) The size of a plum
   b) The size of a clenched fist
   c) About the size of one of your feet

3. WHAT ARE TENDONS?
   a) It's the medical name for fingers
   b) Cord-like structures which attach a muscle to a bone
   c) Fibres which extend along the spinal cord and form part of the nervous system

4. WHAT CAUSES THE PULSE?
   a) It is a wave of pressure that passes along each artery every time your heart beats
   b) It is an expansion of the veins in the arms and neck caused by the movement of the diaphragm
   c) It is a muscle contraction caused by movement of blood in the veins

ANSWERS

1. a - They total half the body weight.
2. b - The heart lies in the chest between the two lungs, but projecting more to the left side than the right. Its weight in a man varies from 280 to 340 grams; and in women, from 230 grams to 280 grams. It's not widely known that the heart continues to grow into old age.
3. b - They are made of bundles of white fibrous tissue and are very strong.
4. a - The pulse rate is usually about 70 per minute, but it may vary in health from 50 to 100. It is quicker in childhood and slower in old age.

The bones

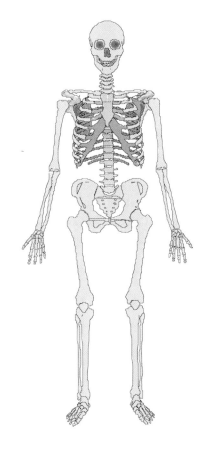

There are some 206 bones in the human skeleton, and they have several functions. As well as giving us our frame, they provide somewhere for muscles to attach themselves. Bones also form a cage, protecting our vital organs, such as the brain, heart and lungs. Blood cells are manufactured in the red bone marrow.

At birth our bones are soft and flexible, and harden as we mature. Children's bones are so elastic, they actually change size throughout the day. After a lot of running about, children shrink in height, but following a period of rest, they regain their full height. Amazing but true!

During childhood we strengthen our bones with calcium, they harden and reach a peak in bone mass between the ages of 20 to 30. The bad news is that from the age of 35 there is natural bone loss in women and men, which speeds up with age. In our latter years they can become brittle. However, research has shown that regular exercise, particularly during childhood, can strengthen bones. Weight-bearing exercise is particularly effective at boosting bone density: this includes activities like walking, running and aerobics.

JOINTS

If you were to try to walk around without bending your knees you would appreciate the importance of our joints. A joint is formed wherever two bones meet, usually where we need some controlled movement. The hands particularly have a wealth of joints, allowing us to accomplish all manner of intricate tasks.

Joints protect themselves with cartilage, fibrous tissue and fluid sacs. Nevertheless, they can be vulnerable and this should be taken into account when exercising. Joints are capable of different types of movement. Ball and socket joints have the most freedom, and the shoulder joint is the best example of this. Others operate like hinges, only capable of bending and straightening, like the elbow.

The muscles

Bones don't move in themselves. For this they need muscles, bundles of fibrous tissue with the ability to contract and pull. For muscles to be firm and healthy they need to be given work. The more you use a muscle the better its strength and tone.

DID YOU KNOW THAT THERE ARE TWO TYPES OF MUSCLES?

SKELETAL MUSCLES

These are the muscles that you can see, when wonderfully toned and defined, in athletes. They are just underneath the skin and make up the outer shape of our bodies. Most skeletal muscles are connected to bones, and it is their shortening and lengthening which enables us to move about. Most skeletal muscles work in pairs: whilst one muscle is shortening in order to bend a limb, its twin on the opposite side of the limb is lengthening to allow the movement.

INVOLUNTARY MUSCLES

These are the muscles involved with our vital organs. They work as if on automatic pilot, and can't be interrupted, except by illness or death. They include muscles in the digestive system, the bladder, the uterus and Fallopian tubes. The most essential involuntary muscle is the heart; like all other muscles, it too benefits from regular, vigorous exercise.

True or False

WOMEN WHO WEIGHT TRAIN END UP LOOKING LIKE MUSCLE-BOUND ARNOLD SCHWARZENEGGERS.

FALSE. Building up muscle bulk is largely dependent on the presence of the hormone testosterone. Men naturally have high levels of this, but the levels in women are much lower. For the average woman, a routine of light weight training will do no more than tone up the muscles and make them stronger, without adding bulk. Of course, there are professional female body builders, but their mammoth muscles are the result of hours of gruelling exercise using heavy weights.

MY MUSCLES ACHE IF I EXERCISE TOO MUCH BECAUSE I HAVE WORN THEM OUT.

FALSE. Muscle ache is due to a build-up of waste products, especially sarcolactic acid, produced by the muscle's activity. The only cure is rest and a relaxing massage. A proper cool-down stretch session will help reduce the risk of soreness. The pain is in fact acting as a warning signal to prevent destructive over-use of a muscle.

The vital organs

Your vital organs love exercise. This is mainly because physical activity means there's more oxygen and less fat whizzing around your body. The two systems that are most directly affected by exercise are the heart and blood circulatory system, and the respiratory system.

THE HEART

The heart is a hollow muscular pump, situated between the two lungs. It has four cavities, each provided at its outlet with a valve, whose function it is to maintain the circulation of the blood. The pumping action of the heart causes the heart to beat. When you exercise your muscles require more blood, so the heart has to work overtime to meet the demand. The fitter the heart, the more blood it can push out with each pump. This means that a well-exercised heart has to beat less to meet increased demand than one belonging to a couch potato.

THE LUNGS

These are a pair of organs in the chest, with the main function of allowing us to breathe. We draw in air through the nose, down the throat and windpipe, and into the lungs via bronchial tubes. We need extra oxygen when we exercise, in particular to nourish large muscles, like those in the legs, the hips, pelvis and arms. At rest about half a litre of air is taken in with each breath by a healthy adult; during vigorous exercise this can go up to about three litres.

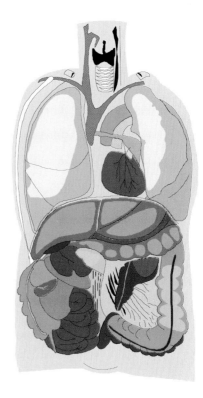

Fitness Flash

The respiratory system is two gallons in volume, and packs a surface area the size of half a tennis court.

The heart beats 40,000,000 times each year. In a typical day it pumps 15 tons of blood around your body.

Why exercise is essential for good health

Each year medical research seems to come up with yet more evidence linking physical exercise with health and well-being. In the early 1990s, experts around the globe reached a consensus on the health benefits of keeping fit. Exercise is one of the best things you can do to reduce your chances of getting seriously ill; it can also help alleviate a whole range of minor ailments. Doctors are now so enthusiastic about exercise, that some health authorities have introduced 'exercise prescriptions'. Instead of writing you out a prescription for drugs, the doctor advises a fitness routine.

Here are the major ways in which exercise can be beneficial:

CORONARY HEART DISEASE

More men and women die from coronary heart disease than any other condition. It's our number one killer, accounting for 29% of all male deaths and 23% of all female deaths. Britain has one of the highest death rates relating to heart problems; six times the rates in Japan. That's the bad news.

The good news is that exercise can radically reduce your chances of heart trouble.

Bev says...

You only get one body. Look after it!

CHOLESTEROL

Coronary heart disease is caused by the narrowing of the heart's arteries by fatty deposits made of cholesterol. Cholesterol is transported in the blood alongside special proteins, called lipoproteins. Those who have coronary heart disease have been found to have high levels of low-density lipoproteins. It is more healthy to have high levels of high-density lipoproteins because these remove cholesterol from the surface of blood vessels. Exercise has been shown to boost the levels of these healthy, high-density lipoproteins.

STROKE

Research suggests that our couch potato life style may be responsible for a significant increase in strokes among middle-aged men. The research is still not clear cut, but the strong suggestion is that exercise may help reduce stroke levels among the wider population too.

CANCER

Physical exercise may help reduce your chance of developing cancers in certain parts of the body. So far, research into this has concentrated on cancer of the colon. A few studies have also found links between exercise and a reduced risk of developing breast cancer, although the research on this is so far inconclusive.

HIGH BLOOD PRESSURE

Blood pressure is greatest at each heartbeat (systolic pressure) and falls between the beats (diastolic pressure). About one in five adults in this country have high blood pressure (i.e. those with systolic blood pressure greater than 159mmHg and/or diastolic blood pressure greater than 94mmHg, and those on drugs to control high blood pressure). Studies show that regular, moderate rhythmic exercise, like swimming and walking, lowers the figures by about 10mmHg in men and women with high blood pressure. It is also suggested that exercise might help the condition from developing in the first place.

DIABETES

Exercise has been shown to help people who have non-insulin dependent diabetes. Research also suggests that exercise may help reduce your chances of developing non-insulin dependent diabetes. For the insulin dependent, keep fit can help prevent the development of cardiovascular disease.

OSTEOPOROSIS

Osteoporosis is a condition in which bones lose their density, become fragile and at risk of fracture. It is a normal part of getting older in both men and women. Osteoporosis is a major health problem in women following the menopause, affecting 30% of women over 50. More women die from hip fractures than are killed by cancers of the uterus, cervix and ovaries combined. There is much research to prove that weight-bearing exercise helps to maintain bone mass.

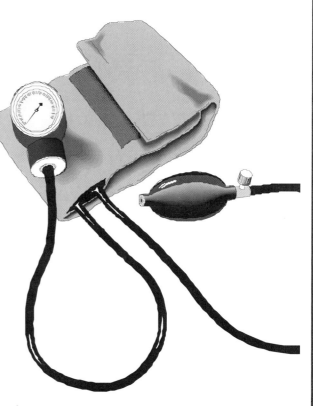

Fitness Flash

If we were all to exercise regularly, it is estimated that the following could be avoided:

Just under one-third of all coronary heart disease. One-quarter of all strokes. Just under one-quarter of non-insulin dependent diabetes in the over 45s. Just over half the hip fractures in the over 45s.

Fat busting!

As a nation we've been steadily putting on pounds for the past fifty years, and during the 1980s the proportion of obese people doubled. Currently, over half of adults are overweight, and 13.5% of men and 17% of women are obese. The trend is likely to continue, despite efforts by the Government to get us slimmer. It is estimated that by the year 2005 about 20% of men and 23% of women will be obese.

It is not exclusively a British problem. The World Health Organisation has described the problem of obesity as a 'world-wide epidemic'. America has the biggest waistline, with over one-third of the adult population sending the scales crashing. An International Obesity Task Force has been set up to tackle the problem.

Thankfully the trend is not irreversible. Exercise is one of the best things we can do to get trim, alongside reducing the amount of fat in our diet. If you want to lose weight, the combination of healthy eating and physical activity is the most effective way of lightening your load.

HERE'S HOW EXERCISE CAN HELP:

- It makes you burn up calories.
- It reduces body-fat levels and maintains lean body tissue.
- It temporarily reduces appetite.
- It helps maintain a higher metabolic rate, even when resting.

True or False

MUSCLE TURNS TO FAT WHEN YOU STOP EXERCISING.

FALSE. Muscle will no more turn to fat than fat can turn to muscle. If you have built up your muscle through exercise, it will simply wither away when you stop working it. It's excess calories that cause fat cells to grow.

Bev says...

There was a time when I got fat. I'd just started *Coronation Street* and had recently given birth. There was no time to exercise, and I put on two stone. I'd gone from teaching 15 classes a week and being in panto to nothing, just sitting in a green room, waiting to do my scenes, eating sandwiches. Watching myself on television I realised I was getting fat; I hated it and knew I had to do something about it.

How fat is too fat?

A woman is classified as obese if she is about two and a half stone over her optimal weight, or, more precisely, has a Body Mass Index (BMI) of 30 or more. A BMI of 20-25 is normal, 25-30 is overweight, 30-40 obese, and above 40 is dangerously obese. A study of over 100,000 American nurses, reported in the New England Journal, found that women with a BMI anywhere above 29 are four times more likely to die from cardiovascular disease than the leanest women; they have twice the risk of cancer (mainly breast, colon and endometrial) and overall mortality. Diabetes, high blood pressure and cholesterol are two to six times higher at this level.

How to calculate your Body Mass Index (BMI)

$$BMI = \frac{Weight\ (kg)}{Height\ (m)^2}$$

For instance, if you weigh 54.5kg (120lb) and are 1.65m (5ft 5in) tall, your BMI will be 54.5 divided by 2.7225 (1.65 x 1.65) = BMI 20.1.

(SEE WEIGHT AND HEIGHT CHART ON PAGE 17)

---

12 REASONS NOT TO BE OVERWEIGHT

If you are overweight:

1. Your chances of developing heart disease increase.
2. You are more likely to develop hypertension.
3. You are more likely to suffer a stroke.
4. There is an increased risk of getting cancer of the breast, uterus, ovaries, cervix and gall bladder in women. Men have higher rates of colorectal and prostate cancers. Those who are severely overweight have higher risks of developing kidney, pancreatic and stomach cancer.
5. Late-onset diabetes has been connected with obesity.
6. You are more likely to get bronchitis.
7. Some fertility problems are connected with carrying too much weight.
8. It increases the risks related to surgery.
9. It contributes to osteoarthritis and joint problems.
10. It causes breathlessness and respiratory problems.
11. Overweight people are more likely to suffer with depression and mental illness.
12. You are more likely to snore.

Fitness Flash

Your racial background could have an impact on your weight. American research shows that Black and Hispanic Americans are more likely to put on weight than White Americans. Asian immigrants to the UK have more 'apple' fat than native Caucasians, and across Europe, Mediterranean women have more 'apple' fat than Northern European women. The differences are likely to be a result of various genetic and cultural factors. (See pages 24 and 25).

Are you the right weight for your height?

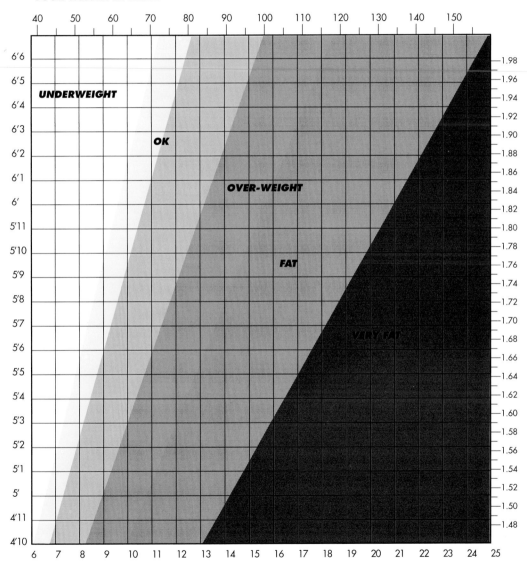

YOUR WEIGHT IN KILOS

40 50 60 70 80 90 100 110 120 130 140 150

YOUR HEIGHT IN FEET AND INCHES

6'6 — 1.98
6'5 — 1.96
6'4 — 1.94 **UNDERWEIGHT**
6'3 — 1.92
6'2 — 1.90 **OK**
6'1 — 1.88
6' — 1.86
5'11 — 1.82 **OVER-WEIGHT**
5'10 — 1.80
5'9 — 1.78 **FAT**
5'8 — 1.76
5'7 — 1.72
5'6 — 1.70
5'5 — 1.68 **VERY FAT**
5'4 — 1.66
5'3 — 1.64
5'2 — 1.60
5'1 — 1.56
5' — 1.54
4'11 — 1.52
4'10 — 1.50

6 7 8 9 10 11 12 13 14 15 16 17 18 19 20 21 22 23 24 25

YOUR WEIGHT IN STONES

YOUR HEIGHT IN METRES

Exercise is good for the mind as well as the body

Exercise won't mend a broken marriage or pay off the overdraft, but it should make you more able to cope with the ups and downs of life. Crucially, exercise makes you feel better about yourself - it boosts your self-esteem.

Psychiatrists typically recommend exercise in the treatment of depression. It can also be helpful in alleviating stress and anxiety, especially a regular rhythmic exercise, like walking and swimming.

There are several theories as to why exercise can help with stress and low moods. Many studies have found that low-intensity, sustained activity like jogging, cycling or swimming triggers the body to produce more endorphins, the body's natural painkillers. When released they produce a sense of euphoria, often called the 'runner's high'. Experts believe that you need at least 40 to 60 minutes of activity to get to this point.

Physical exercise takes your mind off your problems, as an effective diversion. 'Getting away from the problem to exercise can make you identify the nature of your problem and identify the possible solutions open to you,' explains Cary Cooper, professor of psychology at the University of Manchester, Institute of Science and Technology.

According to Stuart Biddle, an associate professor in exercise and sports psychology at the University of Exeter, there are psychological benefits. 'You learn new skills, you can see physical changes in your body, which makes you feel good. You feel in control of your life, and a sense of mastery and achievement.' Meeting goals feels good! As long as you set realistic ones, there's nothing like the sense of achievement to boost the mood.

People who exercise say that it can have a meditative quality which helps them relax. The concentration that can come with a good work-out enables you to really enjoy living in the moment, and stops the racing stress babble in your head of 'things I have to get done'.

Exercise makes us feel more confident about performing physical tasks, and research has also shown that it can improve memory in elderly people. One study that looked at mathematical capability amongst those who exercised and those who didn't, found that the fit ones were quicker and more alert thinkers.

You slip into a super relaxation mode after exercise. 'Your muscles contract a lot when you exercise, then you stop and cool down, have a shower, and the muscles tend to go into extra relaxation to compensate for the activity. It's a pleasant feeling,' explains Stuart Biddle. 'That's why if you exercise at the end of the day, even though you are really tired, you are more alert and comfortably relaxed afterwards.'

Real Results

Sarah Cushnahan, 25, has been a keep-fit enthusiast since she was at school. She works for a firm of accountants, and spends most of her day tied to a desk and a computer. 'Working with figures all day can do my head in,' she says. Sarah works out five times a week, straight after work. 'The gym is near my work, so it's convenient. If I were to drop off home I'd be tempted to stay in. It is hard to stay motivated, but I just say to myself, "I'm going and that's it".' Sarah believes that exercise helps her deal with the stress of her job. 'A good work-out really clears my head and it keeps me going.'

Fitness Flash

The older we are the more inclined we are to take to the couch.
In a major national fitness survey by Allied Dunbar it was shown that:
15% of men and 25% of women aged 16-24,
18% of men and 16% of women aged 25-34,
24% of men and 20% of women aged 35-44,
32% of people aged between 45-64 and
55% of those aged 65 or older, TAKE NO EXERCISE AT ALL.

Fitness Flash

In one psychological study, patients suffering with depression were divided into groups who took up running and groups which had psychotherapy. After ten weeks the runners showed a significant decrease in depression, comparable to the best outcomes obtained with therapy.

Real Results

Correen Thornton, 44, has been a keep-fit enthusiast for the past 20 years. She believes it really helps her deal with her demanding job as an external verifier and training consultant for the awarding body RSA. 'It helps me release all the aggression and pent-up stress I get from working under pressure.' She works out every night after work, three times with Beverley, and also takes a martial arts class and attends a weight training session. 'It makes me feel so much better after a busy day.'

It also helps Correen control her weight. At one point she gained three stone when she moved into a desk job. Exercise has helped her get back down to 8 stone 10lb (she's 5ft 2in). 'As a reward, I got rid of all the old clothes and bought new ones. It was expensive, but well worth the money.'

How else can exercise improve your life?

EXERCISE IS BELIEVED TO BE BENEFICIAL IN:

- *helping the condition of varicose veins*
- *alleviating asthma attacks*
- *improving posture*
- *strengthening the back and reducing lower back pain*
- *reducing pre-menstrual syndrome*
- *alleviating insomnia*
- *stopping smoking*
- *stopping alcohol and drug abuse*
- *improving the complexion*

IT CAN IMPROVE YOUR SEX LIFE TOO!

Psychosexual expert Dr Andrew Stanway recommends a routine of hard physical exercise, other than sex, at least three times a week. 'This helps in keeping slim, tunes up the muscles for sex, makes you feel better generally, and improves your body shape and contours,' he says, 'all of which makes the average person feel better in themselves and therefore more loveable.'

Fitness Flash

Over 40% of men and women cite 'lack of time' as the main reason for not exercising. 37% of women and 24% of men say that not being 'the sporty type' stops them from taking more exercise.

THE CALL OF THE COUCH

One of the biggest enemies to getting fit is a little voice in your head which whispers 'why bother?'. You've got the exercise book, you've bought the gear, you thought you were eager and committed, but maybe you were wrong.

Your body seems to be functioning as it should - you can walk and talk; nothing has dropped off or rattles in an alarming manner. You think you're doing OK. Besides, exercising is hell, and you haven't got the time.

Even the most dedicated fitness enthusiasts are tempted to not bother. The best way to tackle the 'call of the couch' is to work through its enticements one by one. Keep 'The Couch Potato's Excuse Guide to Not Exercising' handy, and refer to it in emergencies!

The couch potato's excuse guide to not exercising

'What's the point of being healthy? We all die in the end anyway.'

Research shows that exercising can reduce your chances of getting major illnesses, like heart disease and strokes. Yes, we have to die in the end, but it can make the business of ageing a whole lot more healthy.

Wouldn't you rather live your life feeling at your physical peak, rather than below par?

'I've heard of people who have dropped dead in the middle of exercising. You never hear of someone popping off whilst watching TV, or buying chips.'

It's true that exercise can be harmful if you overdo things, especially if you have a heart problem. If there is any cause for concern you should consult your doctor before you start working out, and take things slowly. Don't get overly anxious; exercise-induced cardiac death is rare in the general population without underlying disease. Overall, exercise reduces your risk of having a heart attack. Doctors even recommend moderate exercise to people who are recovering from attacks. Studies show that physical activity programmes reduce your risk of death after an attack by about 20%.

'I'm too old and wrinkly. I should treat myself like a museum piece in case I break or wear out.'

You're never too old to feel the benefits of exercise. Sensible and moderate exercise will not cause wear and tear; it has been found to be beneficial in improving an older person's musculo-skeletal function and strength.

'People will curl up with laughter when they see me down the gym decked out in lycra.'

You can exercise at home if you feel self-conscious, or choose a gym where you feel comfortable, and there are people of a similar age and capability to yourself. Who said you had to wear lycra? A baggy T-shirt is just as good.

'I'm never going to look like a Baywatch babe, or one of the Gladiators. I've got bad genes, it's pointless.'

You're suffering with an exaggerated view of the influence of genetics. Think of it like a card game: you might be dealt a rotten hand, but if you know how to play it to your advantage, you could still be a winner.

'Life's too short. I simply haven't got the time.'

If you're worried that life's too short, exercise gives you a better chance of living longer. Exercise will also help you have more time, as it will give you the energy to get things done. You don't have to spend hour upon hour down the gym. One of the brilliant things about exercise at home is that you can do it whenever you have a spare moment, and there's no additional travelling time.

'I do enough exercise already; I took the stairs the other day instead of the lift.'

Research suggests that we tend to over-estimate the amount of physical activity we do.

Staying motivated

Buying and reading this book is the easy bit. Doing your first work-out isn't so tough either. The really difficult thing about getting fit is staying that way. Fitness experts believe that if you can maintain a programme for six months, your likelihood of dropping out diminishes. It gets in the blood after that and starts to become your way of life. Exercise psychologist Stuart Biddle believes the most dangerous time is during the first few months. About 50% of people give up a structured exercise programme by month four. Often it's because they have chosen a class which is too challenging. 'The very unfit people will find it hard going. They feel a bit fat, or embarrassed because they can't do the movements. It's only the really motivated ones who will stay with it,' he says.

Stuart, who has researched exercise motivation, suggests a few simple strategies to keep you inspired:

• **Don't jump in at the deep end.** Start off with a level of exercise which matches your capabilities. If you over-reach yourself you are more likely to feel a failure, and drop out.

• **Remind yourself of the benefits of exercise.** Keep fit is one of the most important things you can do to improve your health, well-being and good looks. You could subscribe to a fitness magazine and make a point of watching anything on television on the subject.

• **Find an exercise partner.** Make a pact with a friend that you will encourage each other. You could work-out together, either in a class or at home. If at the last moment you are feeling lazy and want to give it a miss, it means you would be letting someone down and having to cancel arrangements. It also makes exercise a social event and a whole lot more fun.

• **Monitor your progress.** Use the note pages at the back of this book to chart your progress. It's good to record your weight, measurements, amount and type of exercise, and how it made you feel.

• **Set goals.** Think of short term goals which are very realistic, and then one or two long term goals, which are a bit more ambitious, but still achievable. Use the notes pages to record them, and mark how you are doing. If you are working out at a gym and have an exercise trainer, make sure that you have regular check-ins with them to chart your progress.

• **Make it interesting.** Exercise isn't boring: it's fun and exciting. If you are finding your routine tedious, you're doing it wrong. One of the most common problems is lack of variety. Make sure you change your routine regularly. Break-out now and try something completely different: salsa classes, hill walking, water aerobics, trampolining, whatever.

- **Build it into your life.** One of the best ways to sustain exercise is to build it into the routine of your life. If you find it's impossible to make the aerobics class on a Thursday night, maybe you could cycle to work for a couple of days instead, or go shopping without the car.

- **Reward yourself.** Give yourself a pat on the back when you reach your targets. There's nothing like praise to sustain enthusiasm. You could buy yourself a treat now and then - a new figure hugging dress, a trip to the hairdressers, a great night out. You will have deserved it.

Bev says...

I think that the most difficult thing about exercising is to get it to be a part of your life. Even if you commit to just one class a week, especially if you're a working mother, your whole life revolves around trying to get to the gym for that hour. It takes two or three months to get used to it, and then it becomes part of your life. People I work with on *Coronation Street* wonder how I do it, and where I get my energy from? My job is very tiring and demanding, and I can be there seven days a week when there's a big storyline. I actually have more energy because I work out. There are times when I think it's the last thing I want to do. But I have to go because I'm committed to the people who come to my classes. I get there, and five minutes into exercising I'm not tired at all. I love it!

Real Results

Brenda Lilley, 41, decided to shape up on her fortieth birthday. 'I thought, I can't stop being 40, but I can stop being fat.' Brenda, who is 5ft 1in, was 10 stone 4lb, and spent her life hiding in big baggy jumpers and ski-pants. She attributes her weight gain to age and a change in life style. 'I used to be active, playing netball and rounders, and when the children grew up, I used to watch them do it instead.' She remembers how being overweight made her feel: 'I went to Corfu and felt really self-conscious on the beach. And when I was going out I used to get depressed as my clothes were too tight.' One of the secrets of Brenda's weight-loss success was the way she kept herself motivated. She teamed up with three of her friends and joined a gym. 'It made it a social thing as well, and it didn't feel like hard work. You all encourage each other.' Brenda then joined Beverley's exercise class with her friends. 'Bev's classes are fantastic. Each one is so different and she gives so much enthusiasm and she is so encouraging.'

Brenda enjoyed her holiday a lot more this year. 'We went to Kos and I was 8 stone 1lb. I felt great. My husband said he couldn't believe how well I had done in 12 months.'

Work with what you've got

We all come in different shapes and sizes, and there's nothing you can do to change your basic shape. You can blame or thank your parents for that, because it's from them that you inherit your frame. You can, however, get rid of that extra padding, and tone things up. If there are areas that you think need special attention, there are exercises in this book which can be used to 'chisel' out the shape you want.

We have distorted ideas about the body beautiful, mainly thanks to the media's portrayal of women. However, time and again in surveys on what men find sexy in a woman, they say someone who is fit and feels confident and happy with her body. Being physically attractive means loving what you've got and making the most of it.

TAKE A LOOK AT YOURSELF

Before you start exercising, it's a good idea to take a long look at yourself, naked, in a full-length mirror. If you find yourself cringing at the sight of all the wobbly bits, make a mental note of how you feel. You can bet that you will enjoy looking at your body a whole lot more after a period of exercise.

Look at the way fat is distributed around your body. It varies from person to person, but there are two distinct patterns: apples and pears.

Apples carry their fat around their abdomen. Apples rarely gain much weight on their arms and legs. This is most commonly seen as the 'beer belly' in men, and in the weight gain of post-menopausal women. Research shows that apples have a slightly higher risk of developing heart disease, diabetes and gall

bladder problems. The good news is that apples tend to lose the excess pounds around their tummies fairly quickly.

Your action plan should be to work at toning up muscles around your stomach and waistline.

Pears carry fat around their hips and thighs. The typical British woman is often thought of as pear shaped. Pears rarely thicken at the waistline and above, but makes up for it with what they carry below. There are no health risks specifically associated with this pattern of fat distribution, aside from the fact that it's unhealthy to carry too many pounds.

Pear weight is hard to shift, and you will probably have to get very near your target weight before results really show.

Your action plan should be to work out regularly and especially concentrate on the thighs and buttocks.

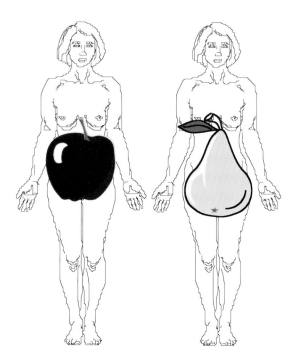

Are you an apple or a pear?

Apples have a higher waist-to-hip ratio than pears. To find out which shape you are, divide your waist measurement by the size of your hips at the widest point. If the ratio is less than 0.85 you are a pear. Over 0.85 you're an apple.

WHAT SPORT SUITS YOUR BODY SHAPE?

Different sports suit different body shapes. The likelihood is that you will best enjoy a sport which you find you are good at. If you weigh 15 stone, you won't be very adept at gymnastics. Or if you are only 5ft tall, your future is bleak as far as basketball is concerned. If you are considering taking up a sport, your best chance of keeping it up is to find the activity which best suits you.

Tall with long limbs:
   SWIMMING, ROWING

Tall and light with long limbs:
   HIGH JUMP, BASKETBALL

Short and powerfully built:
   WEIGHTLIFTING, BOXING, JUDO

Short and light:
   GYMNASTICS, CYCLING

Fitness Flash

The average weight for a British woman is 66.6 kg (10 stone 4lb). For a man it's 78.9 kg (12 stone 4lb). Women tend to carry most weight when they are 55 to 64 years. Men are bulkiest between 35-44 years.

Real Results

Sue Purdie, 45, started doing the Real Results work-out two years ago. Her goal was to lose two stone. 'As you get older you don't realise there's a pound going on here, and a pound there. It just creeps up on you. I was 10 stone 11lb, and only 5ft 1in. I wanted to lose two stone.' Sue remembers how miserable she felt being over-weight. 'Buying clothes was absolutely horrendous, especially with being so small. I felt so tired all the time, and didn't have any energy. Over a ten week period Sue exercised three times a week, watched what she ate, and managed to lose a tremendous one and a half stone. The weight continued to drop off, and has now settled down at a very slim 8 stone 13lb. Sue no longer diets, but maintains her newly-found figure by exercising three times each week. 'I love to go out and buy clothes now. I even swap clothes with my daughter,' she says.

Exercise caution

I t is recommended that you always see your doctor before embarking on a new physical activity programme, especially if you have any health concerns. Exercise is overwhelmingly a good thing for your health, but there are special times when you need to exercise caution.

PREGNANCY

Every pregnancy is different. Some women have more energy than the national grid, others feel tired and sick, or might feel both during different stages. How much exercise you do during pregnancy depends on how fit you were before you conceived. It's certainly not a good time to take up a new vigorous sport, but if you are feeling healthy, there is no reason why you shouldn't continue to follow a moderate exercise programme. If you are able to exercise you will be better prepared for the birth, which is in itself a very strenuous and challenging physical activity.

Don't be over-ambitious during this time. You are more prone to overstretched muscles during pregnancy, so you should take things very gently. It is important to discuss your exercise plans with your doctor or midwife, and to have regular blood pressure checks.

If you want to continue with aerobics, go for the low impact version only, and exercise in a room which is cool and well ventilated. Drink plenty of liquids, and stop immediately if you feel tired or dizzy, experience any pain or shortness of breath. Swimming is one of the best types of exercise during pregnancy. The feeling of weightlessness you get in the water can be a great relief, especially in the last couple of months. Avoid saunas, steam baths and hot tubs.

Vigorous exercise is not suitable for those with a history of two or more spontaneous miscarriages, bleeding in pregnancy, toxaemia or pre-eclampsia, placenta praevia, multiple births or previous problems with the growth of the baby.

POSTNATAL PERIOD

Exercise is recommended a few weeks after giving birth. It is excellent for toning up the muscles which were stretched during pregnancy and delivery, and increasing your energy supply. It may not seem like a top priority when there is a tiny baby to look after, but it really is worth it, especially if you want to get into those jeans again. Ask your midwife to recommend an exercise routine which is specially designed for postnatal women. If you've had a caesarean, wait for four to six weeks before starting to exercise, and check with your doctor first. If you have had a tear or an episiotomy, don't practice stretching exercises until it has healed.

It is especially important at this time to do pelvic floor exercises.

HYSTERECTOMY

If you know you have to undergo any surgery, you should always discuss with your GP whether you need to adapt your exercise routine. The fitter you are the swifter your recovery. 'Good abdominal muscle tone will speed up your recovery,' says Dr Anthony Drake, a GP with a special interest in sports medicine. 'In general it takes about three months to get over a hysterectomy. I would say that you shouldn't exercise for at least four to six weeks to let everything heal inside.'

CHILDREN

It's important that children keep fit. Too many children lead 'lazy' life styles, glued to either the computer or television screen. Their bones are still being formed and their capacity for exercise is different from adults. Exercise allows children the freedom to develop their own games, to explore, play and be kids.
Dr Anthony Drake advises that they don't specialise in any one sport at a young age. 'They should wait until their early teens to narrow it down.'

SENIOR CITIZENS

'Exercise is not ageist,' says Dr Drake. 'Everyone can benefit, but older people should exercise little and often.' He advises that those new to exercise should start off gently. 'Think about stretching and mobility before trying to move too fast and doing pounding exercises.' If you are on any medication, particularly for heart disease and high blood pressure, you should always consult your doctor first.

Real Results

Bev says...

I had a hysterectomy four years ago. Usually you're supposed to take 12 weeks off work. I knew because of the storylines on *Coronation Street* I could only take five. I had to be as fit as I could be before the operation. I was actually back in the gym after 13 days . I painted my toenails the same day after I came out of surgery. The gynaecologist couldn't believe it. The fitter you are the better you cope with anything. *But don't overdo it.* Exercising too much is just as bad as not exercising at all. The rest days are just as important as the exercise days.

Mavis Moxon, aged 66, is Beverley's mum, and each morning goes through a half-hour exercise routine designed by her daughter. 'I've always believed in exercise and healthy eating,' she says. 'It tones me up for the day.' For the past ten years Mavis has been suffering with angina. She believes that the exercise routine and a low fat diet which she has been following for the past four years have really improved her condition. 'It's been tremendous. I was in Whitby a couple of months ago. I went up the steps of Whitby Abbey, and there are quite a lot of them. I didn't have any chest pain or breathlessness. I did it easily.' Mavis does mostly stretching exercises and a short session of step aerobics. 'I stay within my limitations. I couldn't keep going for hours like Beverley does.' Mavis is a sleek size 12, 5ft 6in and weighs 9st 2lb. 'It keeps me trim,' she says. 'I concentrate mainly on my waist, which tends to thicken with age.' Her routine has made Mavis a lot more confident about her health. 'Apart from my six monthly reviews, I don't have to visit the doctor with any complaints.'

WHEN YOU FEEL ILL

'It is dangerous to exercise during acute illness,' warns Dr Drake, 'particularly viral infections like colds and flu. If you have a temperature you shouldn't exercise. You won't get any benefits from it and, taken to extremes, it can affect your muscles.'

EXERCISE ADDICTION

Exercise is a healthy habit to acquire. However, for a small number of people it might become an unhealthy addiction. Exercise addicts are totally consumed by their need to work out. It is the main driving force in their lives and if they are forced to stop they become depressed and anxious; they suffer insomnia and general fatigue. Don't overdo things - you should be able to take a few days off from your work-out routine and put your feet up without feeling remorse.

EATING DISORDERS

Those who suffer with eating disorders have become obsessed with slimming, to the point of starving themselves to achieve the thinnest possible body. Since exercise is connected to weight loss, there may be an unhealthy attachment to physical activity as part of the condition. Anorexia nervosa causes extreme thinness, yet the sufferer will still see herself as grossly fat. She refuses to eat, even though she is ill through lack of nutrition. She will often keep her eating habits secret.

Bulimia nervosa is a similar psychological condition, but the sufferer binge-eats, and then vomits or uses laxatives to control her weight.

Both conditions are most common during puberty. Although they predominantly affect girls, boys can suffer from eating disorders too. Specialist help is needed in both cases.

NO PAIN, NO GAIN. FOR EXERCISE TO BE EFFECTIVE, YOU HAVE TO PUSH YOURSELF UNTIL IT HURTS.

FALSE. Although exercise may be difficult at times, and unpleasant, it shouldn't hurt. Pain and exercise do not go hand-in-hand. When you work-out hard your body actually produces its own pain killers, called endorphins, which naturally mask discomfort.

Real Results

Christine Bretherton, 42, has always tried to keep moderately active, and played netball or rounders once a week. She wanted to try something different, and was keen to tone up her bottom and hips. 'Once you reach 40 to 45, if you're not careful you can look a bit frumpish.' She joined Bev's Real Results class, and has never looked back. 'All my friends say that I'm looking good, and that I don't look my age. I've found I'm buying younger fashions because I feel so much better about myself.' Christine, who is 5ft 4in and 8 stone 10lb, says that she now wears shorter skirts, and 'I don't feel embarrassed in a bikini.'

But best of all, she really enjoys keeping fit. 'It's fantastic. Bev's very enthusiastic and it rubs off on you. I find it gives me so much more energy, which I need with working full time, having a family and a house to run.'

Get Down To It!

This is the chapter where you put theory into practice and start working that body. Use the notes pages at the back of this book to chart your progress, and have fun. But before you get going, assess your fitness rating.

Live wire or sofa slug?

How do you know whether you are a live wire or a sofa slug? Here are a few ways you can test out your fitness levels.

DO YOU:

- Sigh when the lift or escalator is out of order?

- Throw a wobbly because the car is at the garage for a couple of days?

- Drive to pick up a newspaper, even though the shop is just around the corner?

- Panic when a friend invites you out for a swim, walk or cycle ride?

- Groan because you have to change the TV channel without the remote control?

- Own exercise and sporting equipment which is gathering dust?

If you answered 'yes' to any of the above there's a good chance that you need to increase your level of physical activity.

For a more scientific approach, you could take your pulse or try a simple stamina test (see box). Time yourself walking and/or jogging along a flat path, for a distance of one mile, going as fast as you can, without letting yourself get uncomfortably short of breath. It's likely to take between ten to twenty minutes. Here's a rough guide to your stamina rating:

MINUTES TAKEN	STAMINA RATING
10 or less	very fit
10-12	quite fit
12-15	fair
15-20	unfit
20 or more	very unfit

These figures are based on averages for both sexes and all ages. If you are under 35, you are capable of more and should grade yourself in the next category down. If you are over 55, you can grade yourself in the next category up.

Measuring your pulse

The pulse rate is a way of measuring how hard your heart is working, and can be used as a guide to your level of fitness.

You can feel your pulse wherever an artery lies close to your skin. It's easiest to find on the underside of your wrist in line with your thumb. You can also find your pulse under your jaw, just outside the midline on your neck, in the centre of your groin and on the arch of the foot, in line with the big toe.

Feel for your pulse with the tips of the three middle fingers.

Count the number of beats you can feel in 15 seconds. Multiply by four to get the rate per minute.

The pulse rate varies with age. The normal, average resting pulse is 60-80 beats per minute until the age of 40 or so. During mild or moderate exertion, your pulse rate should rise to between 120 and 130. Until you are sure you are fit, you shouldn't exceed this figure during exercise. As you get older, the maximum recommended pulse level diminishes.

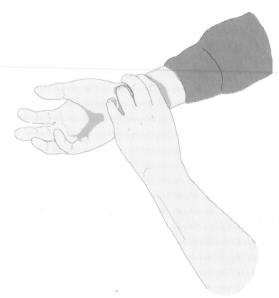

YEARS		PULSE RATE
50-54	-	117
55-59	-	113
60-64	-	109

HOW ARE YOU DOING? PULSE COUNTED IN 15 SECONDS:

UNDER 45 YEARS	OVER 45 YEARS	FITNESS RATING
below 20	below 21	excellent, you're doing brilliantly
20-22	21-23	good, keep it up
23-28	24-29	average, you can do better
above 28	above 29	poor, time to get moving

The gear

You don't have to be all decked out in the latest lycra leotard to get fit - a baggy T-shirt and leggings are fine. The essential items are your bra and shoes. Wear a well-supporting sports bra, especially if you are busty. Choose your training shoes with care - ill-fitting ones, without the right support, could lead to injury. There is a bewildering array of training shoes on the market. Choose a shop where the assistants are well-informed and can help you make the right selection according to your needs.

HERE ARE A FEW TIPS:

- Go for function and comfort rather than style.
- For aerobics you will need a shoe with good lateral stability and reinforced sides. The back of the foot should be higher than the front of the foot. Good front foot cushioning is vital as you spend a lot of time on your toes. Go for a high top to limit ankle sprains.
- Choose good rear-foot control if you suffer from shin splints or knee problems.
- Blisters, aching feet and sore toes are caused by wearing the wrong size of training shoe.
- If you have an old pair of trainers which you have already been using on your work-out routine, you could take them with you to the sports shop to see where you need most support.

Bev says...

I wear a leotard and tights because I have to show off different parts of my body to the class. But if I'm training on my own, I'll wear jogging pants and a big, baggy T-shirt. I like not to be noticed. You've just got to feel comfortable and enjoy yourself.

Some rules to remember when exercising

- Consult your doctor before starting any exercise program - particularly if you haven't exercised in a long time.

- Start with a little exercise and gradually increase the length and intensity of your programme.

- Exercise in a well-ventilated room, clear of any furniture and low-hanging light fittings.

- Start your work-out session well-hydrated, drink plenty of water throughout and drink immediately at the end of your session to avoid dehydrating. If you get thirsty, it's too late!

- If it hurts, don't do it. Check that you have followed all of the instructions and teaching points carefully before proceeding.

- If you experience breathlessness, nausea or overheating, consult your doctor before continuing your programme.

- When exercising, if you experience difficulty coordinating the arms and the legs, just do the legs.

- If you get tired quickly, drop the arms and complete the programme with just the legs.

- Balance your programme - work the whole body each week.

- If you are pregnant, or planning to start or add to your family, let your doctor know that you are currently exercising. He or she may have some guidelines for you to follow or a recommendation not to continue exercising based upon your individual situation.

  - Wear cool, comfortable, well-fitting clothing.

  - For support and comfort, wear a supportive sports bra.

- Wear shoes that are well-fitting, and provide lateral support and cushioning for the feet.

- Never use the bathroom scales to monitor your progress - they never tell you the whole story. When you first start exercising, your body weight may actually increase as you increase your muscle tone whilst simultaneously decreasing your body fat. The way that your clothes fit is always a good indicator of your progress.

- A sensible programme that combines calorie control and an exercise programme will provide sound, permanent results over a period of time. You will not notice changes from day to day. Over a period of weeks however, you will notice wonderful improvements.

Your Complete Work-out

Warm Up

Begin with your feet a little more than shoulder width apart with the back straight, the tummy pulled in and the knees aligned with the feet.

With the arms crossed over and in front of the body, sweep them down and around in a full circle to meet above the head, whilst breathing in.

As the arms are brought down to the starting position, breathe out. Repeat 4 times.

LOWER BACK RELEASE

Pull in the tummy as you bend forwards, supporting your body weight on the thighs, whilst rounding the lower back. Hold for 8 seconds.

Keep the tummy pulled in as you come back to the flat back starting position. Repeat 4 times.

SQUAT TOUCH

Stand with your feet a little more than shoulder width apart, with the back straight, tummy pulled in and the knees aligned with the feet.

Transfer your body weight to the left leg and then to the right leg, tapping the opposite foot as you complete the move. Repeat 4 times with each leg.

STEP TOUCH

From a standing position, step to the right, bringing the left foot in with a toe tap.

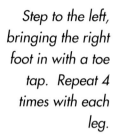

Step to the left, bringing the right foot in with a toe tap. Repeat 4 times with each leg.

EASY WALKS

Step forward with the feet in a wide position and step back, bringing the feet together with a toe tap. Repeat 4 times with each leg.

ALTERNATING SIDE LUNGE

Begin with the feet together and place the right leg out to the side. Return to the centre and repeat with the left leg. Repeat 4 times with each leg.

ALTERNATING KNEE LIFT

Keeping the back straight and standing tall, bring the right knee towards the chest and repeat with the other leg. Repeat 4 times with each leg.

Warm Up Stretches

CALF STRETCH:

(back of lower leg): with feet parallel, arms clasped behind the back, toes pointing forward, push the right heel into the floor and hold for 10 seconds whilst lifting the arms slightly away from the body.
Change sides and repeat.

HAMSTRING STRETCH:

(back of thigh): the right leg is straight with the toes turned up and the other leg is bent at the knee. Support the body weight on the thigh of the bent leg. Hold for 10 seconds then change sides and repeat.

QUADRICEP STRETCH:

(front of thigh): standing on the left leg, using a chair for balance, the right leg is bent at the knee with the foot up behind in the other hand. Push the right foot down into the hand keeping the knees aligned and the pelvis square to the chair. Hold for 10 seconds then change sides and repeat.

UPPER BACK STRETCH:

Wrap both arms around the upper body and pull the shoulder blades apart - it's just like giving yourself a big hug!

NOW ON TO AEROBIC COMBINATION ONE!

Aerobic Combination One

THE WALKS

Walk forward for 4 counts, bringing the hands up under the chin with the elbows out to the side.
Repeat going back 4 counts. Repeat 2 times.

LEG CURLS AND TRICEP KICKBACKS

Begin with legs shoulder width apart, elbows cocked behind the body with the armpits closed and the palms facing inwards

Lift the right leg up behind whilst simultaneously extending the arms behind from the elbow. Return to the starting position.
Change legs.
Repeat 2 times with each leg.

GRAPEVINE

Start with feet together and hands on hips.

Step the right foot to the right.

Travelling to the right,
cross the left leg behind.

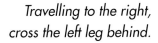

Step the right foot to the right. Close the left foot to the right with a step and a clap! Close the left foot to the right with a step and a clap! Repeat the exercise to the left. Repeat 4 times in each direction.

STEP TOGETHER AND CLAP
Step to the right, left leg close.
Step to the left, right leg close.
Repeat 4 times in each direction.
**Repeat all the
Aerobic Combination One exercises, 4 times.**

NOW ON TO AEROBIC COMBINATION TWO!

Aerobic Combination Two

ALTERNATING FLICK KICKS
Standing with the feet together, jump slightly and kick the left leg forward. Return to the starting position and repeat with the right leg. Repeat 4 times with each leg.

PONYS
Starting with the feet together, skip to the left, right leg touch and close.

Skip to the right, left leg touch and close. Repeat 4 times with each leg.

JOGS
Jog for 4 counts forward and 4 counts back. Repeat 4 times.

TWIST
Twist to the right and then to the left. Repeat 16 times.

Repeat all the Aerobic Combination Two exercises, 4 times. If you're feeling particularly energetic, join both Aerobic Combination One and Two exercises together. Repeat 2 times.

Standing Leg Work

FORWARD LUNGE AND BICEP CURL

Begin from a standing position. Step forward with the right leg, lifting the left heel as you do so.

Drop straight down, bending the front and back knees until they are at right angles. Lift up after reaching your bottom position. Step the feet back together then repeat with the other leg. Repeat 4 times with each leg.

SQUATS

Stand with feet shoulder width apart, arms to the front of the body, with the feet pointing forward. Hips and shoulders are square to the front. Keeping the tummy pulled in and the back flat, bend at the knees and the hips on the way down keeping a slight forward lean. Repeat 8 times.

ALTERNATING SQUATS/ SHOULDER RAISES

Start with the feet together and hands on the hips. Step to the right with the feet pointing forwards.

Raise the arms in front for balance as the buttocks are pushed out behind. On returning to the starting position, squeeze the buttocks as you finish the move. Repeat 8 times.

LUNGE BEHIND

Start with the feet together, stomach in and back flat. Keeping your balance, extend the left leg behind. Then bend the front and back knees until they are at right angles. Lift and return back to the starting position, and repeat on the other side.

ALTERNATING LEG LIFTS

Start with feet together. Step forward onto the right leg lifting the arms. Lift and extend the left leg, squeezing the buttocks. Ensure that the lower back stays still. Lower the left leg and step together. Repeat 4 times with each leg.

Now repeat the Standing Leg Work exercises: 2 x beginner. 3 x intermediate. 4 x advanced.

Side Lying Floor Leg Work

SHORT LEVER

Lying on your left side, lean slightly forward with the legs bent slightly at the hips and the knees, rest your head on your hand.

Keeping the knees and toes pointing forward, lift the right leg slightly then lower it back down again with control. Repeat 4 times on each side.

LONG LEVER

Lying on your left side, lean slightly forward with the legs bent slightly at the hips and the knees, rest your head on your hand.

Keeping the knees and toes pointing forward, lift the right leg slightly higher than in the short lever exercise. Repeat 4 times on each side.

LIFT AND EXTEND

Lying on your left side, lift the right leg which is bent at the knee.

At the top, extend the right leg from the knee before returning to the starting position. Repeat 4 times on each side.

INNER THIGH LIFT

Lying on your left side leaning slightly forward with the right leg bent at 90 degrees at the hip and knee. The left leg is straight with the feet flexed and the toes pointing forward.

Lift and lower the left leg with control. Repeat 4 times on each side.

Repeat all the exercises in the Side Lying Floor Leg Work. 2 x beginner. 3 x intermediate. 4 x advanced.

Face Down Leg Work

LEG LIFTS

Lying face down with the legs extended and the head resting on the back of the hands, raise the right leg.

Keeping the lower back still, the spine aligned, squeeze the buttocks tight before returning to the starting position. Repeat 4 times with each leg.

LEG CURLS

Lying face down with the legs extended and the head resting on the back of the hands, raise the right leg slightly off the floor.

Bend at the knee, bringing the heel towards the buttocks and squeeze the back of the thigh before returning to the starting position. Repeat 4 times with each leg.

LEG LIFT AND CURL

Lying face down with the legs extended and the head resting on the back of the hands, raise the right leg up off the floor.

Bend the leg at the knee and squeeze the back of the thigh. Then straighten the leg before returning to the starting position. Repeat 4 times with each leg.

Repeat the exercises in the Face Down Leg Work: 2 x beginner. 3 x intermediate. 4 x advanced.

Abdominal and Lower back

There are three different levels of Crunch. Choose the level that is most suitable for you.

CRUNCH (BEGINNER)

Lying on your back place one hand behind the head and the other behind the opposite thigh. Use this hand as an aid when you lift up. Now place the other hand behind the head and the other behind the opposite thigh and lift up. Repeat 4 times.

CRUNCH (INTERMEDIATE)

Place both hands behind the head but do not interlace the fingers.

Lift up. Repeat 4 times.

CRUNCH (ADVANCED)

Lying on your back with one arm lifted above the head and the opposite hand placed on the back of this arm to create a cradle of support for the head, lift up. Repeat with the other hand behind your head. Repeat 4 times.

There are three different levels of Reverse Crunch. Choose the level that is most suitable for you.

REVERSE CRUNCH (ADVANCED)

Lying on your back with arms by your side, both legs slightly bent at the hips and the knees and feet in the air.

Bring the elevated legs towards the chest and lift the upper body into a crunch position. Repeat 8 times - rest - and repeat 8 times.

BEGINNERS

Lying on your back with one hand behind the head and the other on the thigh, one leg is bent at the hips and the knee, with the foot on the floor, whilst the other leg is slightly bent at the hip and the knee with the foot in the air. Bring the elevated leg towards the chest as you lift the upper body into a crunch position. Repeat 8 times, then change sides, and repeat 8 times.

INTERMEDIATE

Lying on your back with both hands behind the head, one leg is bent at the hips and the knee with the foot on the floor, whilst the other leg is slightly bent at the hip and the knee, with the foot in the air. Bring the elevated leg towards the chest as you lift the upper body into a crunch position. Repeat 8 times - rest - and repeat 8 times.

There are three different levels of Side Crunch. Choose the level that is most suitable for you.

SIDE CRUNCH (BEGINNERS)

Lying on your back with the right hand behind the head and the elbow to the side, reach down towards the ankle with the left arm, crunching at the waist.
Repeat 4 times on each side.

(INTERMEDIATE)

Lying on your back with knees bent, the left hand behind the head and the elbow out to the side. Reach diagonally across the body with the right arm to just beyond the opposite knee. Repeat 8 times on each side.

(ADVANCED)

Lying on your back with knees bent, cross the right leg over the left, with the ankle resting on the thigh. Place the left hand behind the head with the elbow out to the side and the right arm flat to the side of the body. Bring the left shoulder towards the right knee. Keeping the elbow out, feel the crunch at the waist on the other side of the body. Breathe out on the way up and breathe in on the way down. Repeat 8 times on each side.

SINGLE ARM LOWER‑ BACK RAISES (BEGINNERS)

Lying face down with both arms out in front. Lift the body up from the elbows only, keeping the eyes looking at the floor 12" in front of you.
Repeat 8 times.

(INTERMEDIATE)

Lying face down with both arms out in front, bent at the elbows. Lift the body up keeping one hand in contact with the floor for support, keeping the eyes looking at the floor 12" in front of you. Avoid lifting too high. Repeat 8 times.

(ADVANCED)

Lying face down with both arms bent at the elbows with the head resting on the back of the hands. Lift the body, keeping the eyes looking at the floor 12" in front of you. Avoid lifting too high. Repeat 8 times.

Repeat the Abdominal & Lower Back exercises:
2 x beginner. 3 x intermediate. 3 x advanced.

Cool Down Stretches

Hold each stretch for 15 seconds.

ABDOMINAL STRETCH

Lying face down, push the body up from the elbows pushing the tummy into the floor.

LOWER BACK STRETCH

Balanced on all fours, round the lower back, whilst pulling in the tummy.

UPPER BACK STRETCH

Keeping the hands out in front, pull the body back.

CALF STRETCH

Stretch your left leg out behind and push the heel back from the toes. Repeat with the right leg.

BUTTOCK STRETCH

Extend the left leg behind and across the body. The opposite buttock feels the stretch. Repeat with the right leg.

QUADRICEP STRETCH

One foot up behind, the other leg is out in front and bent at the knee for balance. Repeat on the other side.

HAMSTRING STRETCH

With one leg extended out in front, pull the body back. Repeat on the other side.

INNER THIGH STRETCH

Extend the right leg out to the side, bend the left leg at the knee, keeping that knee aligned with the toes. Repeat with the left leg.

CHEST STRETCH

With the hands placed on top of the buttocks, squeeze the elbows towards one another.

TRICEP STRETCH

Reach the right arm down behind the head and use the left hand to gently push it into the stretch. Hold for 10 seconds. Repeat with the other arm.

With the arms crossed over and in front of the body, sweep them down and around in a full circle to meet above the head, whilst breathing in.

As the arms are brought down to the starting position, breathe out. Repeat 4 times.

Body Blasting Hips, Thighs, Buttocks Work-out

Warm Up

THE WALK

Walk forwards for 4 counts.
Repeat going back 4 counts.
Repeat 2 times.

STEP TOGETHER

Step to the right side, bringing the left foot in with a toe tap.

Step to the left side, bringing the right foot in with a toe tap. Repeat 4 times in each direction.

ALTERNATING HEEL DIGS AND BICEP CURL

Starting with the feet together, dig the right heel forward, whilst simultaneously bringing the forearms to the shoulders. Return to the starting position and repeat on the other side.
Repeat 4 times with each leg.

ALTERNATING LUNGES BEHIND

Starting with feet together, place the arms out in front and extend the left leg behind, tapping the ball of the foot, before returning to the starting position. Repeat with the right leg, keeping the tummy in and the back straight.
Repeat 4 times with each leg.

Stretches

CALF STRETCH:

(back of lower leg): feet parallel, toes pointing forward, push the back heel into the floor and hold for 10 seconds. Change sides and repeat.

HAMSTRING STRETCH:

(back of thigh): the left leg is straight with the toes turned up and the right leg is bent at the knee. Support the body weight on the thigh of the right leg. Hold for 10 seconds then change sides and repeat.

QUADRICEPS STRETCH:

(front of thigh): standing on the right leg using a chair for balance, the left leg is bent at the knee with the foot up behind in the other hand. Push the left foot down into the hand, keeping the knees aligned and the pelvis square to the chair. Hold for 10 seconds then change sides and repeat.

The Work-Out

SQUATS

Start with your feet shoulder width apart with the toes pointing forward. Hips and shoulders are set square to the front.

Keeping the tummy pulled in and the back flat, bend at the knees and the hips on the way down, keeping a slight forward lean. The picture shows the lowest position - avoid going any lower. On returning to the starting position, squeeze the buttocks so as to finish the move.
Repeat 16 times.

PLIES

Start with your feet just a little more than shoulder width apart with the hands on the hips, toes pointing out, keeping the hips, knees and feet aligned. Hips and shoulders are set square to the front.

Keeping the tummy pulled in and the back flat, bend at the knees on the way down, with knees and feet aligned. The picture shows the lowest position - avoid going any lower. On returning to the starting position, squeeze the buttocks so as to finish the move.
Repeat 16 times.

ALTERNATING LUNGES

Begin from a standing position.
Step forward with the right leg,
lifting the back heel as you do so.

Drop straight down, bending the right and left knees until they are at right angles. Lift up after reaching your bottom position. Step the feet back together then repeat on the other side.
Repeat 8 times on each side.

HAMSTRING CURL/BUTTOCK SQUEEZES

On hands and knees with elbows shoulder width apart and knees hip width apart, assume the "thinking position". Lift the right leg with a bent knee off the floor. Raise this thigh until it is parallel with the back, keeping the lower back still. Then return to the starting position keeping the spine aligned.
Repeat with the left leg.
Repeat 8 times with each leg.

OUTER THIGH

Lying on your left side, leaning slightly forward with your legs bent slightly at the hips and the knees, rest your head on your hand.

Keeping the knees and the toes pointing forwards, lift the right leg slightly, then lower it back down again with control. Repeat 8 times with each leg.

INNER THIGH

Lying on your left side leaning slightly forward with your right leg bent at 90 degrees at the hip and knee. The left leg is straight with the feet flexed and the toes pointing forward.

Lift and lower the left leg with control. Repeat 8 times with each leg.

The Cool Down

CALF STRETCH:

(back of lower leg): with feet parallel, toes pointing forward, push the right heel into the floor and hold for 10 seconds. Change sides and repeat.

HAMSTRING STRETCH:

(back of thigh): the left leg is straight with the toes turned up and the other leg is bent at the knee. Support the body weight on the thigh of the bent leg. Hold for 10 seconds then change sides and repeat.

QUADRICEP STRETCH:

(front of thigh): standing on the right leg, using a chair for balance, the left leg is bent at the knee with the foot up behind in the other hand. Push the left foot down into the hand keeping the knees aligned and the pelvis square to the chair. Hold for 10 seconds then change sides and repeat.

Repeat the stretches a second time through and, time permitting, go for a five minute walk!

As your fitness level increases, repeat each section until you can complete the programme three times. Remember that too much too soon could lead to muscle soreness, so progress gradually.

Body Blasting Abdominal Work-out

Warm Up

Reach your right arm over the head.

Pull back 8 times.
Hold for 8 seconds on the final reach.

Repeat with the left arm.
Repeat the exercise 4 times.

LOWER BACK RELEASE

*Pull in the tummy as you bend forward.
Round the back and hold for 8 seconds.*

*Round the back and hold for 8 seconds. Pull the
tummy in as you come back to the starting position.
Repeat 4 times.*

ALTERNATING REACHES

*Reach your right arm over your head
and hold for 8 counts.*

*Now repeat with your
left arm. Repeat 4 times with each arm.*

The Work-out

BASIC CRUNCH (BEGINNER)

Lying on your back place one hand behind the head and the other on the opposite thigh. Use this hand as an aid when you lift up.
Repeat 4 times on each side.

SEE PAGE 46 AND 47 FOR INTERMEDIATE AND ADVANCED CRUNCH INSTRUCTIONS.

SIDE CRUNCH (BEGINNERS)

Lying on your back with the right hand behind the head and the elbow to the side, reach down towards the ankle with the left arm, crunching at the waist. Repeat 4 times on each side.

SEE PAGE 48 FOR INTERMEDIATE AND ADVANCED SIDE CRUNCH INSTRUCTIONS.

REVERSE CRUNCH (ADVANCED)

Lying on your back with arms by your side, both legs are slightly bent at the hips and the knees with the feet in the air.

Bring the elevated legs towards the chest and lift the upper body into a crunch position. Repeat 8 times - rest - then repeat.

SEE PAGE 48 FOR BEGINNERS AND INTERMEDIATE REVERSE CRUNCH INSTRUCTIONS

LOWER BACK RAISES (BEGINNERS)

Lying face down with the arms out in front. Lift the body up from the elbows only, keeping the eyes looking at the floor 12" in front of you. Avoid lifting too high. Repeat 8 times.

This is one complete set of exercises. As your fitness level increases, repeat a second time through and then eventually a third time before moving up to the next level of difficulty, from beginners to intermediate.

The Cool Down

Reach your right arm over the head. Hold for 16 seconds.

Pull back to the starting position.

Repeat with the left arm. Repeat the exercise 4 times with each arm.

LOWER BACK RELEASE

Pull in the tummy as you bend forwards, rounding the back. Hold for 8 counts. Pull the stomach in as you come back to the starting position. Repeat 4 times.

Body Blasting Chest, Back, Arm Work-out

Warm Up

STEP TOGETHER AND CHEST SQUEEZE

Step to the right, left leg close and squeeze the arms across the mid-line of the body. Repeat to the other side.

HEEL DIGS WITH BICEP CURL

Start with feet together and the arms by the side. Dig one heel forward whilst curling the forearms towards the shoulders. Return to the starting position and repeat on the other side.

LUNGE BEHIND WITH TRICEP KICKBACK

Start with the feet together and the elbows cocked behind the body with the armpits closed and the palms facing inwards. Extend the right leg behind, tapping the ball of the foot whilst simultaneously extending the forearms from the elbows. Return to the starting position and repeat with the left leg.

NARROW SQUATS WITH ARM PULL DOWN

Start with the feet together, the tummy pulled in, the back straight and the arms extended overhead.

Bend at the knees, maintaining slight forward lean of the upper body with the shoulders over mid-thigh whilst pulling down the arms in a wide arc. Return to the starting position.

Repeat the Warm Up 4 times then complete the following stretches.

Stretches

TRICEP STRETCH:

Reach the right arm behind the head and use the left hand to gently push it into the stretch. Hold for 10 seconds.

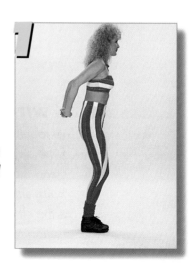

CHEST AND SHOULDER STRETCH:

Clasp the hands behind the back and gently lift the arms. Hold for 10 seconds.

UPPER BACK STRETCH:
Reach forward and round the upper back.
Hold for 10 seconds.

Chest

There are three different levels of push-ups. Choose the level that's most suitable for you and complete 3 sets of 8 push-ups with a 90 second rest in between.

BOX PUSH-UP (BEGINNERS)
Keeping the head and spine aligned and the back flat, the knees are hip width apart and directly below the pelvis.

The hands are shoulder width apart with the elbows slightly bent and the fingers pointing forward. Bend the arms at the elbows on the way down and push back as you straighten the arms and return to the starting position.

MODIFIED PUSH-UP (INTERMEDIATE)

Keeping the head and the spine aligned and the back flat, the knees are hip width apart and behind the position of the pelvis.

The hands are shoulder width apart with the fingers pointing forward. Bend the arms at the elbows on the way down and push back up as you straighten the arms and return to the starting position.

FULL PUSH-UP (ADVANCED)

Keeping the head and the spine aligned and the back flat, the legs are out behind and resting on the toes. The hands are shoulder width apart with the fingers pointing forward.

Bend the arms at the elbows on the way down and push back up as you straighten the arms and return to the starting position.

Triceps

There are three different levels to choose from. Remember to choose the level most suitable for you.

TRICEP (BEGINNERS)

Start with the hands below the shoulders and the fingers pointing forward and the legs bent at the knees at 90 degrees. Extend from the elbows and then return to the starting position.

TRICEP (INTERMEDIATE)

Start with the hands below the shoulders and the fingers pointing forward and the legs extended $^3/_4$ of the way out from the body. Extend from the elbows and then return to the starting position.

TRICEP (ADVANCED)

Start with the hands below the shoulders and the fingers pointing forward and the legs fully extended away from the body. Extend from the elbows and then return to the starting position.

Complete 3 sets of 8 Tricep Dips with a 90 second rest in between each set.

- If you are new to exercise, perform the following moves exactly as in the pictures shown.
- If you are an intermediate exerciser, use 1lb hand weights.
- If you are an advanced exerciser, use 2lb hand weights.

Remember that if you are using weights, maintain control of the arms throughout and if you become tired half way through, put the weights down and continue without them.

N.B. Never use hand weights in the Warm Up or Stretches.

SINGLE ARM ROWS (BEGINNERS)

From a standing position with the left leg bent at the knee and the right leg straight, the upper body weight is supported on the thigh. The working lever is extended below the body. This is the starting position.

Pull the right arm up underneath the shoulder keeping the elbow close to the body. Return to the starting position to complete the move. Complete 3 sets of 8 Single Arm Rows for both the left and the right side of the body with a 90 second rest between each set.

The Cool Down

With the arms crossed over and in front of the body, sweep them down and around in a full circle to meet above the head, whilst breathing in.

As the arms are brought down to the starting position, breathe out. Repeat 4 times.

TRICEP STRETCH:

Reach the right arm down behind the head and use the left hand to gently push it into a stretch.
Hold for 10 seconds. Repeat with the other arm.

CHEST STRETCH:

Clasp the hands behind the back and gently lift the arms. Hold for 10 seconds. Breathe in and out 4 times.

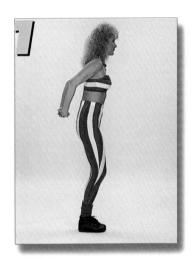

UPPER BACK STRETCH:

Reach forward and round the upper back.
Hold for 10 seconds.
Breathe in and out four times. Relax!

Mind & Body Work-out

Standing with feet apart, reach across the body and pull back 4 times.

Reach over the body and pull back 4 times. Hold for 15 seconds.

LOWER BACK RELEASE:
Pull in the tummy as you round the back, then push the tummy flat as you come back to the starting position. Repeat 4 times. Repeat the first two moves on the other side of the body and repeat the lower back release.

Stand with the feet hip width apart.

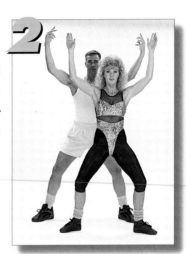

Breathe in and out 4 times with large arm patterns. On the last one gently move into a hamstring stretch.

HAMSTRING STRETCH:

One leg is straight with the toes turned up and the other leg is bent at the knee. Support the body weight on the thigh of the leg bent at the knee. Hold for 15 seconds. From the hamstring stretch, lift up and move into a calf stretch.

CALF STRETCH:

Feet are parallel, toes are pointing forward the spine is aligned. Lift and lower the heel and the arms in a rhythmical motion 4 times. Then hold with the heel pressed into the floor for 15 seconds.

From the calf stretch, move into the hip stretch.

HIP STRETCH:

Lift the heel up, drop the body down and tuck the pelvis under. Hold for 15 seconds. From the hip stretch, move into the quadriceps stretch.

QUADRICEP STRETCH:

Place the weight on the front foot, lifting the other foot up behind towards the buttocks, then press the foot down into the hand. The opposite arm is raised for balance. Hold for 15 seconds. Bring both feet back together and breathe in and breathe out 4 times then repeat the warm up from the hamstring stretch and work the other side of the body.

FOCUS AND CENTRE

Stand with the feet hip width apart.

Breathe in and out 4 times with large arm patterns.

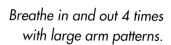

This time breathe in with the hands coming up to the mouth like a cup. Breathe out again, pushing the hands down. Repeat 4 times.

Next take the body weight to one side, bringing one hand up and breathing in at the same time. As you return to centre, breathe out and lower the arm. Repeat 4 times.

Now repeat all the exercises in the Focus and Centre section as one large rhythmical pattern 4 times.

PROGRESSIVE RELAXATION

Lying face up on the floor with the arms down by the side of the body and the legs flat to the floor, breathe in and breathe out 4 times. Tighten all the muscles in the face, hold for 5 seconds then relax. Breathe in and breathe out twice. Tighten all the muscles in the chest, the arms and make a fist, hold for 5 seconds then relax. Breathe in and breathe out twice. Tighten all the abdominal muscles and the buttocks, the legs and point the toes, hold for 5 seconds then relax. Breathe in and breathe out twice. Lying face up on the floor with the arms down by the side of the body and the legs flat to the floor, breathe in and breathe out 4 times.

Continue by repeating in reverse order, back up the body: legs, abdominals, chest/arms, face. Incorporate this Mind & Body Work-out whenever possible - at the office, at the beach, in the garden, in the house. It will not become a work-out for you, but more of an experience to be treasured.

Joining a gym

You can get wonderfully fit working out at home with this book. It is a very comfortable and convenient way of fitting exercise into your life. But there's also a lot to be said for joining a gym, especially if you want to get more advanced in your exercise routine. There you will find professional advice, fun and funky aerobics classes, free weights and variable resistance machinery, possibly a swimming pool and beauty services, and a refreshment area where you can socialise. Bigger places have créches, or exercise classes for children, so the whole family can go along.

Some health clubs are very luxurious, and cost an arm and a leg. Monthly membership instalments can make them more affordable. Local authority facilities come much cheaper, and although they won't be so exclusive, the standards have improved a lot over recent years.

Choosing the right gym can make or break your exercise routine, so here's what to look out for:

WHERE IS IT?

If you are going to sustain your routine the club needs to be convenient, either near your home or place of work. Are there good car parking facilities or public transport connections? Will you feel safe late at night?

WHAT ARE THE MEMBERSHIP DEALS?

A good club will have a wide choice of membership, including cheaper off-peak membership and corporate deals. There may be special rates for families and couples. Check what the fee entails. Do you have to pay any extra for exercise classes? Can you pay in instalments?

DO THE CLUB HOURS SUIT YOU?

A basic but important detail: Is the club open at the times that are most convenient to you? If you need facilities for children, are these available when you want them (or if you want to avoid children, are there times to do so)?

DO YOU FIND THE PLACE COMFORTABLE?

Look around at the people in the gym. Would you feel comfortable joining them? Does the place feel friendly? Ask about social functions and inter-club tournaments - this can be a good

indication of how much effort is made to make things fun. A lively notice board is a promising sign. Did the person behind the reception desk smile and take an interest in you? Working out next to a man who is built like a gorilla can be intimidating. Women-only gyms are popular for this reason. Would you prefer an all female environment? Alternatively, some gyms offer women-only hours.

IS IT CROWDED?

Check out the gym at the time of day when you would use it most. How many people are using the place? The warning signs are people having to queue for machines and facilities, and over-crowded classes. Chat to some of the members and ask them how busy they find the place.

WILL YOU GET GOOD INSTRUCTION?

Check that the instructors are certified - look for BAWLA, NABBA, FFI, RSA, PEA, YMCA or ACSM qualifications or a relevant degree. They should be helpful, encouraging and easy to approach. The good ones will be walking around and talking to members, updating their programmes and encouraging reassessment. There may be a personal training option for an extra cost.

WHAT ARE THE CLASSES LIKE?

A good club will offer a wide variety of studio classes for all levels, ages and abilities. Look at the timetable and see whether it matches your needs. Specialist classes like yoga and antenatal are a positive indication.

IS IT CLEAN AND TIDY?

If you want to get a good idea of a club's standard of hygiene, look in the loos and showers. Balls of fluff around the plughole, unsavoury cubicles and scarcity of toilet paper should all ring warning bells. Check that the pool and spa area are regularly cleaned and monitored - some clubs display test results indicating pH and bacteria levels.

IS THE GYM EQUIPMENT OF A HIGH STANDARD?

The machines should look strong and well maintained. There should be a wide variety to choose from. Check that the club has a service contract to fix things speedily when they break down. There should also be free weights to make your workout more interesting.

WHAT ARE THE CHANGING ROOMS LIKE?

Are they big enough, with adequate locker space? Check out that the showers have power, that there are mirrors and hairdryers. More expensive clubs which offer real luxury will provide fluffy towels and body lotions.

ARE THE REFRESHMENT FACILITIES GOOD?

Water should be free. There may be a café or bar area. Check out the menu. It should offer healthy beverages and foods. Cans of fizzy drinks and burgers are not the sort of thing you want to be eating regularly.

ARE THERE EXTRA SERVICES?

Massage and beauty services may be available. There may be sun beds (although remember these are not healthy for your skin, even though they are often found in health clubs).

The beat goes on

The right music can make all the difference to your work-out. According to one study, if you play upbeat music while you exercise, you'll keep going for 25% longer than without. The secret to choosing the right track is the beats per minute (bpm). A good bpm for a warm-up is about 124 to 128; for low-impact aerobics about 128 bpm; and a high impact workout can soar from 134 bpm to 150 bpm for the ultra fit. For a warm-down, drop to a slower beat of 124 bpm.

7 THINGS YOU NEVER KNEW ABOUT SWEAT:

1. You have an enormous number of sweat glands - 2.5 million of them, scattered over the surface of your skin.
2. You sweat at least one litre each day.
3. When it is hot and you are physically active you can drip up to three litres an hour.
4. Sweating is essential - it maintains your body's temperature.
5. The soles of the feet and palms of the hands are some of the sweatiest parts of your body. It is here you find in greatest numbers the eccrine sweat glands, one of the two types that we have.
6. The other type of sweat gland is called the apocrine, and they don't start perspiring until you reach adolescence. They can be found in all the very personal nooks and crannies: armpits, the anus, genitals and nipples.
7. Sweat in itself doesn't have an odour. BO is caused by bacteria on the skin decomposing the sweat.

Fitness Flash

Research conducted on athletes suggests 6-7pm is the optimum time to exercise. That's the time of day when your body temperature is at its peak, your muscles are most flexible, your stamina and strength is highest and your circulatory system and heart is most ready for exercise.

What is the pelvic floor?

The pelvic floor consists of layers of muscle stretching like a hammock from your pubic bone (the hard bone under your pubic hair), to the end of the backbone. These muscles hold the bladder, uterus and bowel in place. Muscle fibres circle the openings of the urethra, vagina and anus, and act like valves.

A normal healthy pelvic floor is firm and supportive, but it can become damaged. Childbirth plays havoc with it, and lack of exercise and ageing can cause problems. A damaged pelvic floor can lead to stress incontinence. This is when you pee a little bit when you sneeze or cough. It can also cause prolapse of the womb, and loose vaginal walls.

HOW TO DO PELVIC FLOOR EXERCISES

To identify the muscles you are trying to strengthen, stop peeing mid-flow.

EXERCISE ONE

Lying on your back with knees bent and feet on the floor, contract or draw up your pelvic floor, hold for three seconds, relax and repeat five times. Repeat during the day, building up to ten groups of five contractions. Don't overdo it, as it could lead to soreness.

EXERCISE TWO

Imagine you are in a lift, and as you go up, try to draw in the muscles gradually. When you reach your top floor, don't just let go, but move down again, floor by floor. You'll probably find that going down is harder than going up.

THE DISCREET EXERCISE

Some hail it as the exercise which can most improve your sex life. Until recently, women in the West knew nothing of its love-making benefits, whilst elsewhere in the world it was taught to pubescent girls as a normal part of sex education. It is an exercise so simple and discreet that you can do it while standing at the bus stop or washing up, and no one will ever know. As well as improving your sex life by tightening up the vagina, it has numerous other health benefits. It's called the pelvic floor exercise, and it's very easy.

Facial exercises

If you want to bring a youthful glow to your face, try these six facial exercises. Practised every day, they will only take a few minutes, and will really tone up your face and help delay signs of ageing.

NECK MUSCLES & JAW LINE

Tilt your head up slightly - don't pull back. Stick out your chin.

Head still, open mouth, lowering jaw. Lower and lift jaw.

DOUBLE CHIN

Rest chin on your fingers. Reach bottom lip over top lip. Place tip of tongue behind teeth on roof of mouth (not touching teeth).

Press and release tongue. Feel muscle under chin working with fingers.

UPPER EYE
With index fingers - push up eyebrows.

Close eyes using the upper lid - feel the pull.

CHEEK MUSCLES
Place thumbs between back teeth and cheeks. Hold thumbs approx half an inch away from teeth.

Pull cheeks back against resistance of thumbs.

UNDER EYE

Place little fingers on cheekbones and look up without moving head.

Try to close eyes using the lower lids. Feel the resistance against fingers.

FOREHEAD

Place your finger tips around hairline and push back gently but firmly.

Lower eyebrows by resisting against fingers. Lower and release.

You found the book - why not try the video?

You may be interested to know that Beverley Callard's new video,
Rapid Results, her follow-up to the UK's No.1 fitness video Real Results,
is now available at video stockists.
Rapid Results: VC6566   Real Results: VC 6516

Shape Up Your Life

Getting your body into shape will make you look and feel fantastic, but if you want the best Real Results you need to shape up your life style too. This means looking at what you eat, how you relax and how you deal with stress. People often find that exercise and healthy living go hand in hand; you start out just wanting to shed a few pounds and one thing leads to another. But always remember, living healthily doesn't mean you have to become a sanctimonious misery. The most important thing is that you enjoy life, and if that means having the occasional indulgence, go for it!

Food, glorious food

Food is fuel, and we can't expect to be great performers if we put low grade petrol in our tanks. So what foods should we eat for optimum health? We seem to be bombarded with so much conflicting advice that it's hard to know what to put in the supermarket trolley. The fantastic news is that healthy eating doesn't mean boring eating, or having to give up anything you like. It may mean clambering out of a junk food diet rut, using your imagination when you cook, and cutting down on some types of food. As always, it's a matter of balance.

GETTING THE BALANCE RIGHT

One of the first steps towards healthy eating is getting the balance of your diet right. Different food groups provide different nutrients, so they need to be eaten in the right proportions. One of the easiest ways is to imagine your day's food intake on a plate. Around one-third of the plate is filled with starchy carbohydrate foods, such as bread and rice, and another third is filled with fruit and vegetables. The remaining third is made up mostly from protein foods like fish, pulses, eggs and meat, dairy produce, and a small amount of fatty and sugary foods.

ENERGY BOOSTING CARBOHYDRATES

BREAD...PASTA...RICE... POTATOES...CEREALS...LENTILS

Starchy carbohydrates are rich in fibre but low in fat, which means they are filling but not fattening. Most of us need to eat more of these foods: they should provide about 50-70% of our calories, which is about twice as much as the average person eats. Choose wholefood versions which have a higher level of fibre. That means brown bread and rice, wholemeal pasta and flour, and muesli or bran rather than refined breakfast cereals.

Fibre, or roughage as it used to be called, doesn't sound very appetising. It conjures up grim images of sawdust and cardboard, but it can be tasty. It comes from the cell walls of fruits, vegetables, grains, shoots, leaves and nuts, and provides us with the soft bulk needed to ease the passage of food through the digestive system. It helps reduce the risk of colon cancer and improves bowel movements. Few of us get enough fibre. On average we eat about 12g of fibre a day, but we should be eating 18g.

Bev says...

If I go out for a meal I'll eat what I want, and then the next day I'm good again. You shouldn't torture yourself for having had a treat.

VITAL FRUITS AND VEGETABLES

FRUITS...SALAD...VEGETABLES...

Never skimp on the amount of fruits and vegetables in your diet, which should make up a third of your food intake. The Government recommends that we eat at least five servings of fruits and vegetables a day (not counting potatoes), although some people believe that the levels should be higher for optimum health. Different fruits and vegetables have different health benefits, so go for variety. Those of an orange colour, such as apricots and pumpkin, are good sources of betacarotene and vitamin C - important disease fighting antioxidants (antioxidants counter the effects of damaging chemicals called free radicals). Dark green leafy vegetables also contain high levels of iron and calcium, needed for healthy blood.

Go for fresh or frozen fruit and veggies and eat raw when possible. If you are cooking, steam or microwave, or stir fry in a tiny amount of oil. Boiling vegetables can strip them of valuable vitamins.

PROTEIN POWER

BEANS...LENTILS...NUTS...TOFU... SEEDS...TEXTURED VEGETABLE PROTEIN...EGGS...QUORN...FISH... SEAFOOD...POULTRY...RED MEAT

Proteins are found in the cells of plants and animals, and foods rich in protein should make up about 15% of your total daily calories, that's around two portions a day.

Generally we rely too much on animal sources of protein, which are high in cholesterol and saturated fats. When you eat meat, choose chicken and turkey rather than red meat, as it is lower in fat, especially if the skin is removed. But if you want red meat go for the leanest cuts and in small quantities.

Fish and seafood is a healthy option as it is high in protein but low in fat. Fish can be classified into white or oily varieties. The oils in white fish, like cod and coley, are concentrated in the liver, while those in oily fish, like mackerel and tuna, are spread throughout the flesh. White fish are the lowest in fat, whilst oily fish have essential fatty acids that protect against heart disease.

What, no meat?

3 HEALTHY MEAT REPLACEMENTS

Tofu, also called bean curd, doesn't look or taste very exciting; but it is superb nutritionally, being high in protein and minerals, low in fat and with no cholesterol. Tofu is a food staple in the East, made from curdling warmed soya bean milk, then pressing it until it becomes solid. Happily, it absorbs flavours easily and marinated or smoked tofu are also available. It can be added to stir fry dishes, stews and casseroles. Silken tofu has a runny consistency and can be used in creams and dips.

Textured vegetable protein (TVP) is a processed soya bean product available in dehydrated form as mince or chunks. It can take on the texture of meat when cooked, but is lower in fat and much cheaper. Not a tasty option on its own, it takes on the flavour of the juices in which it is cooked. Look out for handy, ready-prepared packets of bolognaise and chilli sauces that use TVP.

Quorn is a relatively new arrival on the supermarket shelves, produced from a tiny plant related to the mushroom family and grown through a process of fermentation. It is mixed with egg white to bind it, flavoured and made into chunks or mince, which have a texture amazingly similar to meat. It is an excellent source of protein, B vitamins, and, unusually for a protein food, also contains fibre. It is very low in fat and contains no cholesterol. Critics point out that Quorn is not made using free-range eggs.

DAIRY DELIGHTS
MILK…CHEESE…YOGHURT… FROMAGE FRAIS

Dairy foods are an important source of calcium, protein, vitamin A and vitamin B12, and until the 1980s had a pristine, healthy image. Then concerns began to creep in about the high fat content in dairy produce and we all had to think again. Due to the high levels of saturated fat in milk, care needs to be taken over its inclusion in our diet. Weight for weight cheddar cheese contains six times as much saturated fat as sirloin steak. The dairy industry has fought back with a whole range of low-fat products, which are certainly the best choice for adults. Opt for skimmed milk, low-fat yoghurts and low-fat cheeses. Save the double cream for those occasional moments of wickedness.

Fats: friend or foe?

We are all now fully aware that fat can be bad for us, and that we need to cut down on it. However, labelling fat as the dietary villain is over-simplistic. We need fat in our diet, not only to promote energy, but to carry the fat-soluble vitamins A.E.D and K, and to contribute the essential fatty acids our bodies need. Fats maintain healthy bones and skin, help the blood to clot properly and give us good eyesight. Additionally, a diet that is virtually fat free would be very dreary.

Currently about 42% of our calories come from fat, and this needs to be reduced to 30-35%. For women, this means eating about 70g per day, and for men 90g.

THE LOW-DOWN ON FAT

Foods contain mixtures of saturated, monounsaturated and polyunsaturated fatty acids.

SATURATED FATS

These are found mainly in foods of animal origin: meat and dairy produce. They are also in a few plant oils: palm oil, coconut oil and hardened vegetable oils. You can also find them 'hidden' in pastries, pies and cakes. Most of us eat too many saturated fats, which have been connected with high cholesterol levels. Butter contains 55% saturated fat, 20% monounsaturated fat and 3% polyunsaturated fat.

UNSATURATED FATS

There are two types of unsaturated fats - polyunsaturated and monounsaturated. Polyunsaturated fats are the good guys as far as the heart is concerned. The richest sources of polys are from plant seeds and fish - products like sunflower oil, safflower oil, soya oil, corn oil and fish oils. Monounsaturates are found in olive, peanut and rapeseed oils.

TRANS FATS

To make matters even more complicated, there are also the trans fats. These are artificially produced by a chemical process which hardens vegetable and fish oils called hydrogenation. It is thought that may affect blood cholesterol in a similar way to saturates, so it is best to keep the consumption of these fats to a minimum.

French Fries

Are you a salt-aholic?

DO YOU...

- Put salt on your food at the table, before you taste it?
- Add salt to boiling vegetables?
- Eat lots of crisps and salted snacks?

If you answered yes to any of the above you may have become a salt-aholic. You are not alone; we have become something of a nation of salt addicts. Salt is added to processed foods as a cheap way of boosting flavour, and we often habitually sprinkle it on food before even tasting it. As a result, we eat far more salt than we need, and have become accustomed to strong salty flavours. On average we eat about 9g (2 teaspoons) of salt a day, but need only 6g, much of which is naturally present in food. Eating too much sodium, most of which we get from salt, can lead to high blood pressure, which in turn can cause heart disease, kidney disease and strokes.

HERE ARE SOME GOOD WAYS TO CUT BACK ON SALT:

- Add less salt to cooking.
- Get out of the habit of adding salt to food at the table, at least until you have tasted it first.
- Cut down on salty snacks like crisps and peanuts.
- Avoid processed foods, or look out for those which are marked 'no added salt'.
- Flavour foods with lemon juice, herbs, spices and vinegar instead of salt.
- Use low-salt substitutes (although these won't wean you off the salty taste).

Fitness Flash

Fibre gets things moving! In rural Africa the average time taken for food to pass through the digestive system is about 36 hours. In Britain it varies from about three days in young people to as long as two weeks in the elderly. Rural Africans eat four or five times as much fibre as people in the UK.

Sugar is not so sweet

There's very little to be said about the merits of sugar; it is the major cause of tooth decay and contains only calories, with virtually no other nutrients. We don't need sugar for energy; we can get all the energy we need from other foods. Sugar is a carbohydrate which contains a lot of calories in a small volume, so things like chocolate are not filling and easy to over-indulge on. The average chocolate bar contains the same calories as a dinner of chicken, boiled potatoes, vegetables and gravy. It may taste heavenly, but chocolate will neither fill you up nor provide good nutrition.

10 WAYS TO LICK THE SUGAR HABIT

1. Obvious but true - don't keep supplies of sweets or biscuits in the house.
2. Eat a good breakfast - this will prevent the eleven o'clock hunger attack.
3. Keep some healthy nibbles near to hand, like fruit, raw carrots or dried apricots.
4. Analyse what times of the day you usually eat sweet things, and be prepared to break the habit, either by changing your activity or finding a healthy alternative snack.
5. Always buy products which are low in sugar - avoid sweetened cereals and tinned fruit in syrups. When buying jam look out for reduced sugar versions, or jars of fruit purée with no added sugar.
6. Look out for added sugar hidden in processed foods, like tomato ketchup, cans of soup, and even tinned meat.
7. When buying soft drinks choose unsweetened fruit juices, and dilute them with water or soda. Read the small print on drinks labels. Avoid those which call themselves fruit 'drinks', as they usually have added sugar. Look out too for 'spring water with a hint of...' which can be high in sugar despite the healthy marketing.
8. When cooking, try halving the amount of sugar in recipes. It works for most things, except jam, meringue and ice cream.
9. Gradually cut down on sugar in your tea to wean yourself off the sweet flavour. Your taste palate will adjust and one day you'll find it hard to believe that you ever enjoyed such a sickly brew.
10. Can't resist eating some sweets? Look out for sugar-free confectionery.

Healthy eating for kids

Growing children need masses of energy, and they need the same sort of varied balanced diet as grown, ups, with not too much sugar and with fats in moderation. Children under two years old need whole milk. Between the ages of two and five years, provided they are eating a good varied diet, you can introduce semi-skimmed milk. Skimmed milk can be introduced from the age of five. Children shouldn't be overloaded with fibre, especially if they are under two years old. Give them the same types of wholefoods as the adults, but in scaled down amounts. Encourage children to snack on foods such as wholemeal bread and fruits, plain popcorn, breadsticks, yoghurts and Twiglets. Save sweets and fizzy drinks as occasional treats, given after a meal if possible.

Daily vitamin and mineral guide

VITAMIN A

Found in: liver, cheese, eggs, carrots, green leafy vegetables, oily fish (avoid liver and vitamin A supplements during pregnancy).
Recommended amount: women 600mcg, men 700mcg.
Needed for: growth and cell development; vision and immune function; healthy skin and mucous membranes.

VITAMIN B1 (THIAMIN)

Found in: brown rice, wholegrain cereals and breads, peas, seeds and nuts, Brewer's yeast, molasses, pork, liver, heart, kidneys.
Recommended amount: women 0.8mg, men 1mg.
Needed for: obtaining energy from carbohydrates and fats; prevents the build-up of toxins in the body.

VITAMIN B2 (RIBOFLAVIN)

Found in: spinach, green leafy vegetables, eggs, wholegrains, brown rice, meat, fish, molasses, Brewer's Yeast, milk, yoghurt.
Recommended amount: women1.1mg, men 1.3mg.
Needed for: the release of energy from food and for the functioning of vitamin B6 and niacin.

VITAMIN B6

Found in: meat, fish, poultry, eggs, nuts, bananas, avocados, wholegrains, yeast extract, soya beans.
Recommended amount: women 1.2mg, men 1.4mg.
Needed for: the release of energy from proteins; immune function; the nervous system; formation of red blood cells.

VITAMIN B12

Found in: meat, poultry, fish, eggs and dairy products, fortified breakfast cereals.
Recommended amount:1.5mcg for both women and men.
Needed for: the making of DNA and the white sheath that surrounds nerve fibres; cell division.

VITAMIN B3 (NIACIN)

Found in: nuts, eggs, meat, fish, pulses, fortified breakfast cereals.
Recommended amount: women 13mg, men 17mg.
Needed for: the production of energy in cells; the formation of neurotransmitters; healthy skin; an efficient digestive system.

VITAMIN C

Found in: fresh fruit and vegetables, especially blackcurrants and oranges.
Recommended amount: 40mg for both women and men; smokers are advised to have 80mg.
Needed for: healthy bones, teeth, gums, cartilage and skin; makes neurotransmitters, an important antioxidant; aids absorption of iron from plant food.

VITAMIN D

Found in: fish liver oils, eggs, fortified margarines, tuna, salmon, sardines.
Recommended amount: enough vitamin D is made when your skin is exposed to sunlight. If you are confined indoors you'll need 10mcg.
Needed for: the absorption of calcium and phosphorus for healthy bones and teeth.

VITAMIN E

Found in: vegetable oils, wheatgerm, nuts, seeds, margarine.
Recommended amount: women 3mg, men 4mg.
Needed for: the prevention of oxidation by free radicals of polyunsaturated fatty acids in cell membranes and other tissues.

FOLIC ACID

Found in: leafy green vegetables, milk, citrus fruits, wheatgerm, bread, liver, kidney.
Recommended amount: 200mcg for both women and men. An additional 400mcg supplement should be taken by pregnant women and those planning to conceive.
Needed for: cell division; the formation of DNA and proteins in the body.

IRON

Found in: meat, nuts, eggs, fortified cereals, beans, green leafy vegetables.
Recommended amount: women 14.8mg, men 8.7mg.
Needed for: the production of haemoglobin in the blood and enzymes involved in energy metabolism.

ZINC

Found in: oysters, red meat, peanuts and sunflower seeds.
Recommended amount: women 7mg, men 9.5mg.
Needed for: normal growth, reproduction and immunity, aids the action of many enzymes.

POTASSIUM

Found in: avocados, fresh and dried fruit, particularly bananas and citrus fruits, seeds and nuts, potatoes and pulses.
Recommended amount: 3500mg for both women and men.
Needed for: fluid and electrolyte balance within cells; a regular heartbeat and normal blood pressure; the transmission of nerve impulses.

MAGNESIUM

Found in: wholegrain cereals, wheatgerm, pulses, nuts, sesame seeds, dried figs, green vegetables.
Recommended amount: women 270mg, men 300mg.
Needed for: bones and teeth; assists in nerve impulses; important for muscle contraction.

CALCIUM

Found in: sardines, soya products, milk, yoghurt, cheese, sesame seeds, green leafy vegetables.
Recommended amount: 700mg for both women and men.
Needed for: the building of bones and teeth; nerve transmission; blood clotting; muscle function.

ESSENTIAL FATTY ACIDS

Found in: sunflower oil, evening primrose oil, green leafy vegetables, fish oils, walnuts, rapeseed oil, mackerel, herring.
Recommended amount: No Government recommendation.
Needed for: boosting calcium uptake; regulation of hormones; protects against heat disease.

PHYTO-OESTROGENS

Found in: soya beans and soya products, alfalfa, ginseng, celery, fennel, linseed.
Recommended amount: No Government recommendation.
Needed for: the rebalancing of hormones.

Lightening your load the healthy way

Many of us are so desperate to slim we will try any crazy diet which comes on the market. No matter how convincing or novel these slimming gimmicks are, the sad truth is that weight control means a permanent change in eating habits. Research shows that there are genetic factors which determine our bulk (medical experts can't agree a figure on the influence of genetics: it varies between 5 to 50%.) Even if it is in our genetic make-up, our 'fat genes' only give us the predisposition to put on weight if our life style is too inactive and our diet too high in calories. Change your eating and exercise habits and you'll shed pounds.

Obesity experts agree that the best type of diet to follow is one that reduces your intake of fat. 'Fat is the most energy dense nutrient. The number of calories in a gram of fat is more than twice the number of calories in a gram of protein or carbohydrate,' says Dr Susan Jebb, head of obesity research at the Medical Research Council's Dunn Clinical Nutrition Centre. 'Cutting the fat allows you to reduce the calories whilst maintaining the bulk of your diet, so you feel full.' Dr Jebb suggests that a loss of 2lb each week is sustainable.

Although crash diets in books and magazines promising weight loss of 7lb a week sound brilliant, there are several important reasons why we should banish them to the bin.

1. It's very difficult to ensure that you are getting all the nutrients you need on a highly restrictive diet and you'll probably feel ill and miserable.

2. Your metabolic rate (the rate you burn up your calories) goes down when you diet - just what you don't want. But of course, it's nature's way of conserving your resources. 'The more rapidly you lose weight the more rapidly your metabolic rate will go down,' says Dr Jebb.

3. You also lose the wrong type of weight. 'When people lose weight rapidly a larger proportion of it will be lean tissue. When you lose weight slowly your body is drawing almost exclusively on your fat stores to provide the extra energy you need,' says Dr Jebb.

Women should not aim to have less than 1,000 calories a day, and men 1,500.

Fitness Flash

Children with two obese parents have about a 70% risk of becoming obese compared to less than 20% in children with two lean parents. This could be explained by life style factors. However, studies of adopted children have revealed weight patterns similar to their natural parents rather than their adopted parents.

Fat burning

Exercise has an important role to play in weight control as it helps you maintain your muscles and ensures that you only lose the bit you want to lose - the fat. Exercise is especially important when you have finished dieting and want to keep the pounds from creeping back on. 'There are a lot of studies which show improved weight control in exercisers. The systems that help us maintain our weight seem to operate better in people who have a slightly higher level of physical activity,' says Dr Jebb.

20 WAYS TO CUT DOWN ON FAT

1. Substitute beans and pulses for meat in casseroles, or one of the meat substitutes.
2. Mince is very high in fat. When you cook it, drain off the fat. This can reduce the fat content by 40%.
3. Use less cheese in sandwiches by grating it, rather than using slices.
4. As an alternative to fat-heavy roast potatoes, part boil them and lightly brush with vegetable oil, then crisp in the oven.
5. Fry only occasionally, and when you do make sure the oil is really hot before you put in the food. Use kitchen roll to drain the food before serving.
6. When eating out, choose plain boiled rice with Indian and Chinese food rather than fried rice.
7. Instead of buying ice cream, go for frozen low-fat yoghurt, which can have one-third less fat than an ordinary vanilla ice cream (and is tastier).
8. If you want to eat cake, the lower fat choices are: scones, muffins, fruit buns and malt loaf.
9. Use low-fat yoghurt instead of cream with your deserts. You can also use it as a cream substitute in cooking. Mix a teaspoon of cornflour into a small carton of yoghurt to stop it curdling when heated. Alternatively, add it to hot dishes just before serving.
10. With dishes like beans on toast, do away with a spread - you won't even notice its absence.
11. Make salad dressings with natural yoghurt, herbs, spices, tomato juice, vinegar or lemon juice rather than using mayonnaise or salad cream.
12. Grill, microwave, steam or bake fish rather than deep frying in batter. Grill fish fingers and fish cakes rather than frying them.
13. Choose skimmed milk, which has only 0.6g of fat per pint, rather than whole milk, which has 22g of fat per pint. Alternatively compromise on semi-skimmed with 9g of fat per pint.
14. Have several meat free dishes each week, and eat fish at least twice. Have only tiny portions of lean meat, and keep red meat for special occasions.
15. Choose half-fat cheeses and cottage cheese instead of full-fat hard cheese. Try curd cheese instead of cream cheese.
16. Most fruits are low in fat, but not all. Moderate the amount of avocados you eat. Each one has 8.3g of fat, which is about half a cup. Coconut contains a massive 14.1g of fat.

17. Don't add oil to pasta when boiling. You can stop it sticking with a regular stir.

18. Meat products like sausages, burgers and meat pies are very high in fat. Save for special occasions, and look out for lower fat alternatives.

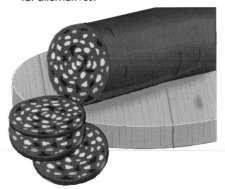

19. Deli meats like salami and pepperoni sausage are very high in fat, often exceeding 70% of the content. Save for special days.

20. Go for oven-ready chips if you need a chip fix. Or if you want to make your own, cut them up big and chunky and pat with kitchen roll before serving.

True or False

BUYING PRODUCTS LABELLED 'LOW-FAT' OR 'LITE' WILL GUARANTEE YOU A HEALTHY LOW-FAT DIET.

FALSE. You must read the small print on the back of the label. There are currently no legal definitions for terms like 'low fat'. For example, a low-fat spread could be 40% fat, while a low-fat yoghurt could only be 0.5% fat. There is a voluntary code of practice, which is not always adhered to. In practice, the term 'low-fat' can differ depending on the context.

Real Results

Marie Holmes, 38, is an actress and long-time friend of Beverley's. It was seeing herself on television that made her decide she had to shape up. 'I did a couple of episodes of *Emmerdale*, playing a nurse, and when I saw myself on screen I absolutely died. I looked gross.' Marie is 5ft 2in and weighed 13 stone. 'I'd had two children by Caesarean and kidded myself it was still post-natal bulge, two years later. I felt unwell and drained of energy, carrying all that weight around; I felt really bad about myself.'

Bev persuaded Marie to join her aerobics class. That was two years ago, and Marie has never looked back. 'It didn't feel like exercise, it was fun.' She started to lose a little weight, but it was when Bev suggested she go on the Hay Diet that things really started moving for Marie. 'It was tremendous. When Bev first explained it to me, I thought "this is a lot of rubbish". I'd tried every sort of diet - you name it. Nothing had worked. But I found this one easy to do. The others involved weighing and measuring, and faddy foods. This was something I could fit into my family meals, which is important when you're running a home. If I had a really busy day I'd have my carbohydrate meal at lunch time, and my protein meal in the evening. If I came back from a class and I was starving, I'd have a piece of wholemeal toast with Marmite on it, no fat.'

Marie has now got her weight down to 9½ stone, and looks and feels fantastic. 'My thighs used to rub together when I walked. There are times now when I catch sight of myself in a mirror and think, "Are those really my slim legs?"

What a difference a Hay makes?

Dismissed by the scientists as a gimmick diet, with no hard medical evidence to prove its worth, The Hay Diet is nevertheless a very healthy and easy eating plan. It was developed by an American, Dr William Hay, who believed that proteins and carbohydrates should not be eaten together because they require different conditions for digestion: an acidic environment for proteins, and an alkaline environment for carbohydrates. Critics say that his theories underestimate the sophistication of the digestive system, but people on the Hay Diet report feelings of increased energy.

Dr Hay recommended that the diet should include four times more of the foods that raise the level of alkali in the blood, than those which raise its acid levels. This means a greater proportion of vegetables, salads, fruit and milk in ratio to animal proteins, nuts, carbohydrates and citrus fruits.

THESE ARE DR HAY'S GOLDEN RULES:

- Carbohydrates should not be eaten with proteins and acidic fruits.
- Vegetables, salads and fruits form the bulk of the diet.
- Proteins, carbohydrates and fats should be eaten only in small amounts.
- Refined and processed foods should be avoided.
- Leave four hours between meals of different foods.

Dr Susan Jebb is cynical about the food combining claims of the Hay Diet, explaining that 'You do not lose weight because of some magical metabolic effect of separating protein and carbohydrate. You lose weight because you eat less.' She does however rate it as a useful way to re-examine your eating habits and modify the excesses, and some people may find it makes dieting more interesting. She does have a word of caution: 'The experience we have of observing how people put this diet into practice is that they tend to have their main meal as usual and cut out the carbohydrate. The consequence is that they end up with a diet that is high in protein and fat, and low in carbohydrate. We don't think it maximises their chances of losing weight.'

Here's how you might plan a typical day's menu according to Dr Hay:

Breakfast: Fresh fruit, small carton of natural yoghurt sprinkled with wheatgerm or mixed nuts, herb tea and fruit juice.

Lunch: Portion of meat, fish, eggs or cheese, salad or vegetables (not potatoes), followed by an apple or orange.

Dinner: Jacket potato or wholemeal bread, with butter, salad or vegetables, fresh figs with fromage frais.

Bev says...

I thought the principles of eating carbohydrate and protein separately made sense, so I tried this diet. Normally when I've eaten lunch, by half past three my tummy has swollen up and I feel tired. After two weeks I stopped getting that bloated feeling, and I didn't get a slump in the afternoon.

Food for thought - Recipes

Starters:

This soup can either be served as a starter or with a roll as a light meal. Broccoli is high in vitamin C and a bowl of this soup will count towards the recommendation of five daily portions of fruits and vegetables.

BROCCOLI SOUP

Serves 4
90 calories, 1g fat, 3g fibre per portion

400g/14oz broccoli
115g/4oz onion
1.25l/2^1/$_4$ pints water
2 chicken or vegetable stock cubes
40g/1^1/$_2$ oz skimmed milk powder
50g/2oz very low-fat fromage frais
Salt and pepper

Break broccoli into florets and slice stems. Slice onions. Put in a pan with water and stock cubes. Bring to the boil then simmer for 20 minutes. Allow to cool, then purée with skimmed milk powder and fromage frais. Season to taste with salt and pepper. Return to pan and gently reheat before serving.

Oily fish is thought to have special health benefits, in particular helping to reduce the risk of coronary heart disease. Serve this pâté as a starter with vegetable sticks or melba toast (no butter needed), or use to make lunch time sandwiches. One portion will fill two sandwiches, rolls or bagels and can be frozen.

KIPPER AND TUNA PATE

Serves 8
100 calories, 5.5g fat, 0g fibre per portion

200g/7oz packet boned kipper fillets
with butter
100g/3^1/$_2$ oz can tuna in brine, drained
200g/7oz carton half-fat soft cheese
5ml/1 teaspoon lemon juice
5ml/1 teaspoon paprika

Cook kippers according to instructions on packet. Discard skin and put fish with its juices in a food processor. Add tuna, soft cheese, lemon juice and paprika. Blend together. Divide between eight small ramekin dishes and leave in refrigerator for at least an hour before serving. Garnish with a sprig of watercress or chopped parsley.

Main Courses:

You really don't need to add anything else to this tasty, quick to prepare meal. If you wish, though, you can serve with a slice of crusty bread or crisp iceberg lettuce. Omit the gammon to make a vegetarian meal and sprinkle extra cheese on top.

LEEK AND GAMMON TAGLIATELLI

Serves 4
435 calories, 7g fat, 4g fibre per portion

115g/4oz lean gammon
450g/1lb leeks, trimmed weight
275ml/ 1/2 pint skimmed milk
15ml/1 tablespoon freshly chopped basil
50g/2oz half-fat, full flavour Cheddar cheese
Salt and pepper
450g/1lb fresh tagliatelli with herbs and garlic

Grill gammon well, discard any fat and cut the lean into small pieces. Slice leeks and put in a saucepan. Cover with boiling water and cook for 10 minutes. Drain. Heat milk, add basil and grated cheese, then season to taste. Stir in gammon and leeks. Cook tagliatelli in boiling water for 3 minutes until just tender. Drain, then toss with leeks and sauce. Serve immediately.

Chicken is an excellent, low-fat meat which is very amenable to many sauces and flavourings. You could use skinless turkey breasts for this dish, too. If you are a vegetarian, substitute chicken with Quorn. Boost your fibre by serving with a helping of boiled brown rice, or a baked potato.

SPANISH-STYLE CHICKEN

Serves 4
225 calories, 8g fat, 2g fibre per portion

4 skinless, boned chicken breasts, 150g/5oz each
1 green pepper
1 medium onion
115g/4oz carrots
1-2 cloves garlic
75ml/3floz water
400g/14oz can chopped tomatoes
15ml/1 level tablespoon freshly chopped thyme or 5ml/1 level teaspoon dried thyme
15ml/1 level tablespoon freshly chopped parsley
Salt and pepper
25g/1oz olives stuffed with pimento

Put chicken breasts in the bottom of a casserole dish. Deseed pepper and cut into strips. Place on top of chicken. Chop onion and garlic and slice carrots. Put in a saucepan with 75ml/3floz water. Bring to boil and simmer covered for 10 minutes until vegetables are just tender, then boil off water, stirring to make sure vegetables do not stick. Stir in tomatoes and herbs, then purée in a food processor. Pour over chicken breasts. Cover and cook at 180°C/350° F/gas mark 4 for 30 minutes. Add halved olives. Cook uncovered for a further 20 minutes.

Rainbow trout varies enormously in size, but this kebab is best using chunky fillets from a large fish. At certain times of the year only small spinach leaves will be available, so if this is the case, use several small ones to surround the fish. This kebab also works with fresh salmon fillets. Serve with boiled rice mixed with boiled peas, or a salad.

PINK TROUT KEBAB WITH DILL MARINADE

Serves 4
200 calories, 8g fat, 1g fibre per portion

450g/1lb rainbow trout fillets
Bunch fresh dill
60ml/4 tablespoons lemon juice
10ml/2 teaspoons olive oil
5ml/1 teaspoon coarse sea salt
16 button mushrooms
16 cherry tomatoes
1 large yellow pepper
16 large spinach leaves

Remove skin from fish, then cut each fillet lengthways down the middle. Divide the trout into 16 pieces. Put into a dish and scatter chopped dill on top. Mix lemon juice with oil and salt. Pour over fish and leave to marinate in the refrigerator for 2 hours, stirring occasionally. Leave mushrooms and tomatoes whole and cut pepper into squares. Wash spinach leaves and put a piece of fish into the centre of each then roll up to form a parcel. Using 4 large or 8 small skewers start with a whole tomato, then thread on fish, mushroom and pepper alternatively along each skewer. Put in a foil-lined grill pan and brush with any remaining marinade. Grill under a medium heat for 3-4 minutes on each side until fish is cooked.

This vegetarian dish can be enjoyed by everyone. Red-skinned onions give a pretty colour, but the regular sort can be used instead.

POTATO, ONION AND COURGETTE GRATIN

Serves 4
390 calories, 18g fat, 4g fibre per portion

550g/1¼lb new potatoes
225g/8oz red-skinned onions
350g/12oz courgettes
1 clove garlic
Salt and pepper
4 medium tomatoes
5ml/1 teaspoon dried mixed herbs
225g/8oz Edam cheese, vegetarian or standard
150g/5oz carton half-fat soft cheese

Scrub the potatoes but do not peel. Cut into thin slices. Thinly slice onions and courgettes. Put potatoes and onions into a pan with crushed garlic and 75ml/3floz water. Cover and simmer gently for 8 minutes, stirring from time to time to prevent sticking, adding a little extra water if necessary. Add courgettes and cook for a further 10 minutes, or until vegetables are tender. Boil off any remaining liquid by leaving the pan uncovered. Stir in the thickly sliced tomatoes and herbs and season to taste. Put half the vegetables at the bottom of a large shallow dish. Dot the soft cheese over the top with half the Edam. Top with remaining vegetables and the remainder of the Edam. Bake at 230°C/450°F/gas mark 8 for 15 minutes.

Puddings:

Ice cream can be a low-fat dessert, but home made versions are sometimes tedious to make. This dessert is quick, easy and delicious. The only disadvantage is that you can't refreeze the ice cream, so make just enough for the meal.

BANANA ICE CREAM

Serves 4
190 calories, 6g fat, 1g fibre per portion

4 medium bananas (approx. 400g peeled)
30ml/2 level tablespoons creme fraiche, light
90ml/6 tablespoons skimmed milk
60ml/4 level tablespoons mini chocolate flakes

Peel bananas, cut into slices and put in a container, then freeze. Just before ready to serve, put bananas in a food processor with creme fraiche and skimmed milk. Blend until creamy in texture. Put into four serving dishes and sprinkle with chocolate flakes. Serve immediately.

Half Spoon sugar is now usually available in supermarkets and is a mixture of sugar and sweetener. It is twice as sweet per spoonful as the equivalent amount of sugar, which means you can use half as much and save calories. If you like a tart apple base then you can use ordinary sugar for the same calories, or increase the sugar to 30ml/2 level tablespoons and increase the calories to 210 per portion. Fat and fibre will remain the same.

EVE'S PUDDING

Serves 4
180 calories, 3g fat, 3g fibre per portion

450g/1lb cooking apples, peeled and cored weight
15ml/1 level tablespoon Half Spoon sugar
5ml/1 teaspoon ground cinnamon
50g/2oz wholewheat flour
2 eggs, medium size
50g/2oz caster sugar

Thinly slice apples. Put in a saucepan with 45ml/3 tablespoons water. Cook gently for 5 minutes until soft but still holding their shape. Put apples in the bottom of an soufflé dish and stir in sugar and cinnamon. Separate eggs and whisk whites until stiff. Add yolks and sugar and whisk until thick. Carefully fold in the flour, then pour on top of apples. Bake at 200°C/400°F/gas mark 6 for 35-40 minutes until golden brown on top and springy to the touch.

Red alert

There are things in life that are far worse for you than enjoying a ciggie, a night on the booze and a stiff cup of coffee. However, if you are serious about shaping up your life and having the best possible health, warning bells should ring in your head whenever those three troublemakers are around.

ALCOHOL

Happily, alcohol can be good for you in moderation; the occasional drink is associated with a decreased risk of coronary heart disease in older men and women. However, in excess alcohol can mean major health problems. It is also fattening; half a pint of beer contains about 90 calories, and an average glass of medium white wine is 95 calories. Alcohol also makes you feel full, so if you are regularly drinking instead of eating a proper meal, you could be missing out on valuable nutrients.

High intakes of alcohol have a long list of health hazards, not least of which is alcohol addiction. If you really care about yourself, you'll keep your consumption to a moderate level.

HERE ARE A FEW TIPS TO HELP:

- Eat before you drink, so that you don't miss out on essential nutrients.
- Try low-alcohol drinks as an alternative.
- Make your drink go a long way with a low-calorie mixer.
- Don't gulp it all down at once. Practice the art of drinking slowly.
- If you have been out on the town, don't drink for 48 hours afterwards (forget hair of the dog).
- Beware of salty snacks whilst drinking as they'll make you more thirsty.
- For a change, arrange to meet friends in places where you know alcohol isn't on offer.

HOW MUCH ALCOHOL IS SAFE?

In general, women can drink up to two or three units a day, without significant risk to health, and men can drink up to three and four units

One unit of alcohol = half a pint of beer....or a small glass of sherry....or a small glass of wine...or a single measure of spirit.

SMOKING

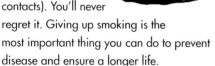

Unlike alcohol, smoking has nothing going for it. Smoking is particularly a problem amongst women at the moment, who apparently find it harder to give up than men. But now, with increasingly more help at hand, quitting is easier than ever. Try anything: patches, gum, support groups, hypnotism, whatever it takes (see the back of this book for contacts). You'll never regret it. Giving up smoking is the most important thing you can do to prevent disease and ensure a longer life.

CAFFEINE

Tea and coffee are both stimulants which work on the heart and central nervous system, and they can become addictive. You are not going to drop dead if your intake is too high, but you might suffer with tremors, sweats, palpitations, sleeplessness and migraine.

Caffeine is also found in chocolate and in some cola drinks. The recommendation is that we drink no more than six cuppas a day (less for people with high blood pressure or kidney disease, and women who are pregnant or breast feeding). A cup of tea has 50-80mg of caffeine, whilst coffee can soar to 200mg. A can of cola might have 43mg-75mg.

Fitness Flash

Tobacco smoke contains over 4,000 different chemicals, many of which are harmful. Nicotine, carbon monoxide and tar are three components of smoke which affect our body and cause disease.

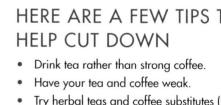

HERE ARE A FEW TIPS TO HELP CUT DOWN

- Drink tea rather than strong coffee.
- Have your tea and coffee weak.
- Try herbal teas and coffee substitutes (like Barley Cup) for a change.
- Try caffeine-free teas and coffees - you might not notice the difference.

Cool it!

Periods of peace and quiet can be hard to find, especially if you have a demanding job, demanding children, a demanding relationship, or all three! But quiet time should be seen as more than just a luxury - it's a fundamental human need. Time to ourselves gives us the opportunity to reflect on our lives and recharge our batteries. If you don't get enough relaxation time, you will feel stressed. This can manifest itself in a number of ways; you might feel anxious, tense, tired, nervous, tearful, unhappy, short tempered and powerless.

A BALANCE OF MIND AND BODY

So far we have dealt with the conditioning of your physical self, but the psychological self also needs to be conditioned so as to minimalise the effects of stress, resulting from a hectic life style.

Popular exercise programmes only touch upon our psychological needs. If you consider that the stretch component of any schedule accounts for less than 20% of the programme, then it is easy to see that there is an imbalance in mind:body fitness.

Answer the following questions to assess how stressful your life style is:

A. When was the last time that you spent 30 minutes relaxing by yourself?

Yesterday	4
Last Week	3
Last Month	2
On Holiday	1

B. How often do you have to rush from one appointment/task to the next?

Almost Never	4
Once/Day	3
Twice/Day	2
Always	1

C. When you exercise, do you ever skip the stretch section?

Never	4
Occasionally	3
Nearly Always	2
Always	1

D. How often do you feel you are caught up in a merry-go-round?

Never	4
Sometimes	3
A Lot	2
Always	1

E. When was the last time that you felt totally content, centred and focused?

Yesterday	4
Last Week	3
Last Month	2
Last Year	1

Add your scores together and check your rating level:

16 or more: You appear to have a well-balanced life style. In fact if you are not a lady of leisure, then you should be. Read on, you are sure to enjoy this next section.

10 to 15: Not bad, you seem to find a balance, then loose it, find it again and so on. It is now up to you to create that balance once again and keep it. A balance of mind & body is important to you, and this next section will help you maintain that balance.

9 or less: Slow down, take a deep breath and count to 10. Start to schedule in breaks as well as appointments, sit in a comfortable room with a cup of tea and some soft music playing, then read on and try this new mind & body programme.

WHAT EXACTLY IS STRESS?

A little bit of the stress reaction is an excellent thing. It's a self-preservation mechanism, popularly known as the fight, flight or freeze syndrome. It's our natural alarm system which helps us deal with dangerous and difficult situations. At such moments our bodies undergo a mass of intricate physiological changes; adrenaline speeds up our heart rate, raises the blood pressure, releases essential body nutrients, causes muscle tension, nerve activation and alert breathing. The trouble begins when we are perpetually in an aroused state, and our hormone system is working overtime. Too much stress can be detrimental to our health, and a whole range of diseases have been related to it.

STRESS-PROOF YOURSELF

There are some stressful things in life that can't be changed, but you can impose damage limitations.

- Keep your working life in balance. Avoid working more than ten hours each day, and make sure you have at least one and a half days off each week, away from routine work. Take a holiday; build regular get-aways into your yearly routine.
- Have some 'Me Time' each day. Even if it's only 10 minutes, build some time into your day which is just for you, when you

can be quiet and alone. Take a relaxing bath at the end of the day, get into the habit of meditating for a brief period each morning, or taking a lunch time stroll.

- Exercise. Keeping physically fit is brilliant for mental well-being. Perform the exercises in this book regularly and you'll notice a difference!

- Nourish yourself. A well-nourished body will stand up to the rigours of life much better than one which is not. Avoid alcohol and cigarettes as quick-fix ways to unwind.

- Don't change too many things in your life at once. You will need some constant stability if you are going to cope with changes in your life; avoid too much upheaval all at once. Changing your job, your house, your relationship and going through a personal transition of some kind is far too much; do things one at a time. If multiple changes are impossible to avoid, make sure there is at least one thing that remains constant, even if it's just your exercise routine.

Bev says...

I'm a worrier and get very stressed. It goes straight to my throat; it gets sore and I suffer with swollen glands. I also went through a stage when I couldn't sleep. I had just started work on *Coronation Street* and had a small baby at home. I was so busy, I'd stopped exercising. In the end I was so tired I couldn't function properly. When I started exercising again and got into a regular pattern, my good night's sleep came back.

Stress Related Diseases

ABDOMINAL PAIN
ACNE
ALCOHOLISM
ALLERGIES
APNOEA (BREATHLESSNESS)
ARTHRITIS (RHEUMATOID)
BACKACHE
CANCERS
CANDIDIASIS (THRUSH)
COLDS
CONSTIPATION
DIARRHOEA
DRUG ADDICTIONS
ECZEMA
GALL STONES
HEADACHES
HEART ATTACKS
HYPERVENTILATION
IMPOTENCE
IMMUNE SYSTEM DEPRESSION
INCONTINENCE
INDIGESTION
INSOMNIA
IRRITABLE BOWEL SYNDROME
MENSTRUAL CONDITIONS
MIGRAINES
NEURALGIA
NEURO-DERMATITIS
PHOBIAS
PREMENSTRUAL SYNDROME
PSORIASIS
SHINGLES
SKIN ERUPTIONS
STROKES
ULCERATIVE COLITIS

Take control

If there are things that are constantly stressing you out, which you know you have the power to change, then do it. If you have problems at work, make an appointment to discuss things with your superior. If you are constantly rowing with a friend or family member, make a commitment to improve the relationship - meet up and sort things out. You may be pleasantly surprised at how easy it is to improve things once you put your mind to it. If the situation doesn't improve, at least you'll know you did your best to resolve the problem.

Live for today. For the most part, try to live in the present and concentrate on the tasks at hand. There is nothing you can do to change the past, and tomorrow will take care of itself.

Finish things off. Always finish off one job completely before starting another. It's much more satisfying, and you won't be left worrying about loose ends.

Learn to say no. Don't take on the impossible; only agree to do what you know you can happily cope with. That includes saying no to unreasonable demands made on you by friends, family and work colleagues.

Be a good communicator. Learn to express your thoughts and feelings clearly and openly, and always listen carefully to what others have to say.

Get support. If you feel overloaded, don't be afraid to ask for help. Family and friends are often pleased to rally round, so don't be too proud to ask.

Take up a creative hobby. Find something you enjoy which is creative rather than competitive, something which helps you to express yourself. You don't have to be brilliant at it, just enjoy it.

Don't ignore deep-seated emotional difficulties. Listen to those long-time difficult feelings which have been nagging away at you and causing anxiety. There may be old hurts from your past which you need to address in order to move on. Talk to a close friend or get professional counselling (see back of book for contacts). You will not feel truly at peace until you have dealt with such problems.

Stress

In 1967, two American doctors, T.H. Holmes and R.H. Rahe, published a list of the most common life event stresses, assessing the degree of anxiety they each evoked. Here's the top ten, in order:

1. **Death of your husband/wife or partner**
2. **Divorce**
3. **Marital separation**
4. **Going to prison**
5. **Death of a close member of the family**
6. **Illness or injury**
7. **Marriage (even the happy events can be stressful)**
8. **Loss of a job**
9. **Reconciliation with marriage partner**
10. **Retirement**

QUICK FIXES WHEN YOU'RE FRAZZLED

If you feel at the end of your tether, there are lots of ways in which you can find immediate relief. If you can build some of these practices into your life on a regular basis it will stop the initial build up of stress.

• Learn to Meditate.

Meditation is an ancient and very effective way of calming yourself, which with practice is fairly easy to accomplish and available to all. There are lots of different ways to meditate and different schools of thought as to which is the best. For beginners, the easiest techniques are those which involve concentrating on your breathing.

Find a quiet room and sit comfortably, loosening any tight clothing. You don't have to sit cross-legged or kneel on cushions, unless you find it comfortable. Candles or fresh flowers help create a conducive space. It is important to keep your back straight, as it will help you stay alert. Relax your face, and shut your eyes. Then simply count one hundred breaths, very slowly, in and out. Follow a normal breathing rhythm, and concentrate on the air, from the place where it touches your nose and moves down your nasal passages, to the rise and fall of your diaphragm. When you have reached 100, start again, until you feel you have had all you need. Given time and practice you will find that you experience a deeper state of relaxation.

• Try Musical Relaxation.

Prepare yourself in a similar way as you would for meditation and become aware of your breath. When you are settled, put on a favourite piece of relaxing music. Try to breathe into the music, allowing yourself to absorb the entire melody. The effect of music is so powerful it can raise or lower your blood pressure, affect your respiration, digestion and muscle tension.

• Treat Yourself to a Massage.

Authentic massage, sometimes called therapeutic touch, is a natural remedy for stress, and one of the oldest and most respected forms of healing. There are many books and short courses on the market which can teach you the basics. For a treat, you could book a professional massage for yourself. Always go through one of the professional bodies to ensure you have a practitioner who is properly qualified (see back for contacts).

There are several different types of massage. Aromatherapists use essential oils when they massage (usually Swedish style). This 'fragrance medicine' helps to restore well-being and prevent illness.

Swedish masseurs rub, knead and drum your muscles with the sides of their hands, often using talc or oils.

Shiatsu practitioners press your body with their fingers and hands, rather than rub. It is based on the oriental belief that there are hundreds of surface points along the body's energy paths (meridians) which can be stimulated to restore balance. It's good if you are body shy, as you don't have to take your clothes off.

Reflexology is massage of the soles of the feet. Practitioners believe that different pressure points on the soles are connected to various parts of the body, and that general health can be improved by gentle stimulation.

- Stay Positive.

There's a lot of truth in the old adage that laughter is the best medicine. Happiness is an attitude, something that you can consciously cultivate. You have a choice to either view the proverbial glass as half empty or half full, and being an optimist will make life a whole lot more fun.

INSTANT BLUES BUSTERS

- Laugh.

Stress consultant, Robert Holden, has run NHS-funded laughter clinics, in which patients suffering with depression are encouraged to laugh. The therapeutic benefits of one minute of genuine laughter are thought to be the equivalent to 45 minutes of deep relaxation.

- Dig out your photo albums.

A new form of cognitive therapy uses the recollection of happy memories to treat depression. Photographs can remind you that you've had happy experiences, and signal that there are more to come.

- Keep a diary.

Many therapists ask their clients to keep a diary of their thoughts and feelings as a way of pinpointing the emotional aspects of their lives, and as an aid to growth and change.

- Sing a song.

Music therapists believe that there's nothing like opening your vocal chords to create a sense of well-being.

- Buy some new clothes and treat yourself to a make-over.

It may sound superficial, but it's one of the easiest ways to boost self-esteem because it reinforces the fact that you are worth tending to.

- Try 'happy breathing'.

Our breathing is shallow when we are upset. Try breathing in deeply and slowly.

- Help others.

It's true that in giving we receive. Knowing that we are useful can be a source of deep pleasure, making us feel connected to the world.

Yearly Work-Out Plan

As you follow the programme, tick off each of the work-outs as you complete them. We have varied the programme with activities that you can do on your own, with a friend or even with the family. Happy exercising!

January

MON	TUES	WED	THURS	FRI	SAT	SUN
OFF	Video: Rapid Results 2 Work-out	OFF	Real Results Complete Work-out	Mind & Body Work-out	OFF	OFF
Video: Real Results 1 Work-out	OFF	Video: Rapid Results 2 Work-out	OFF	Real Results Complete Work-out	OFF	OFF
OFF	Body Blasting Abdominal Work-out	OFF	Body Blasting Hips, Thighs, Buttocks Work-out	OFF	Body Blasting Chest, Back, Arm Work-out	OFF
Mind & Body Work-out	OFF	Relax with a face mask	OFF	Go swimming for 20 minutes	OFF	OFF
Body Blasting Abdominal Work-out	OFF	Body Blasting Hips, Thighs, Buttocks Work-out	OFF	Body Blasting Hips, Thighs, Buttocks Work-out	OFF	OFF

February

MON	TUES	WED	THURS	FRI	SAT	SUN
Mind & Body Work-out	OFF	Try a massage	OFF	Go swimming for 20 minutes	OFF	OFF
Video: Real Results 1 Work-out	OFF	Video: Rapid Results 2 Work-out	OFF	Real Results Complete Work-out	OFF	OFF
OFF	Body Blasting Abdominal Work-out	Body Blasting Hips, Thighs, Buttocks Work-out	Body Blasting Chest, Back, Arm Work-out	OFF	Mind & Body Work-out	OFF
Video: Real Results 1 Work-out	OFF	Video: Rapid Results 2 Work-out	OFF	Real Results Complete Work-out	OFF	OFF
OFF	Body Blasting Abdominal Work-out	Body Blasting Hips, Thighs, Buttocks Work-out	Body Blasting Chest, Back, Arm Work-out	OFF	Go swimming with the family	OFF

March

MON	TUES	WED	THURS	FRI	SAT	SUN
Take a week off - you've earned it!						
Video: Real Results 1 Work-out	OFF	Video: Rapid Results 2 Work-out	OFF	Real Results Complete Work-out	OFF	OFF
OFF	Body Blasting Abdominal Work-out	Body Blasting Hips, Thighs, Buttocks Work-out	Body Blasting Chest, Back, Arm Work-out	OFF	Go swimming with the family	OFF
Mind & Body Work-out	OFF	Relax with a face mask & massage	OFF	Go swimming for 20 minutes	OFF	OFF
Body Blasting Abdominal Work-out	OFF	Body Blasting Hips, Thighs, Buttocks Work-out	OFF	Body Blasting Chest, Back, Arm Work-out	Go swimming with the family	OFF

April

By now exercise has become a very important part of your life. Your body has started to experience a number of changes, your clothes fit differently and people are noticing how great you look. You even have more energy and a greater balance in your life. As the weather gets warmer, some activities will find their way outdoors, so remember the sun block!

MON	TUES	WED	THURS	FRI	SAT	SUN
Video: Real Results 1 Work-out	OFF	Video: Rapid Results 2 Work-out	OFF	Real Results Complete Work-out	OFF	OFF
OFF	Tennis with the girls	Go for a 20 minute Power-Walk	Go swimming for 25 minutes	OFF	Mind & Body Work-out	OFF
Body Blasting Abdominal Work-out	OFF	Body Blasting Hips, Thighs, Buttocks Work-out	OFF	Body Blasting Chest, Back, Arm Work-out	OFF	OFF
Mind & Body Work-out	OFF	Relax with a face mask & massage	OFF	Go swimming for 25 minutes	OFF	OFF
OFF	Tennis with the girls	Go for a 20 minute Power-Walk	Go swimming for 25 minutes	OFF	Mind & Body Work-out	OFF

May

MON	TUES	WED	THURS	FRI	SAT	SUN
Video: Real Results 1 Work-out	OFF	Video: Rapid Results 2 Work-out	OFF	Real Results Complete Work-out	OFF	OFF
Go for a 20 minute Power-Walk	OFF	Go swimming for 25 minutes	OFF	OFF	Cycling with the family	OFF
OFF	Body Blasting Abdominal Work-out	Body Blasting Hips, Thighs, Buttocks Work-out	Body Blasting Chest, Back, Arm Work-out	OFF	Mind & Body Work-out	OFF
Video: Real Results 1 Work-out	OFF	Video: Rapid Results 2 Work-out	OFF	Real Results Complete Work-out	OFF	OFF
Go for a 20 minute Power-Walk	OFF	Go swimming for 25 minutes	OFF	OFF	Cycling with the family	OFF

June

MON	TUES	WED	THURS	FRI	SAT	SUN
Take a week off - you've earned it!	Facial	Massage	Body Wrap	Manicure	OFF	OFF
Video: Real Results 1 Work-out	OFF	Video: Rapid Results 2 Work-out	OFF	Real Results Complete Work-out	OFF	OFF
OFF	Body Blasting Abdominal Work-out	Body Blasting Hips, Thighs, Buttocks Work-out	Body Blasting Chest, Back, Arm Work-out	OFF	Cycling with the family	OFF
Go for a 20 minute Power-Walk	OFF	Go swimming for 25 minutes	OFF	Go for a 20 minute Power-Walk	OFF	OFF
Body Blasting Abdominal Work-out	OFF	Body Blasting Hips, Thighs, Buttocks Work-out	OFF	Body Blasting Chest, Back, Arm Work-out	Go swimming with the family	OFF

July

W ow, now even your husband/partner has noticed the difference in you. You will start to buy different clothes now as your confidence increases. You look in the mirror and you can see the changes as well as feel the firmness of you hips, thighs and buttocks. The weather is still warm, so some of the work-out will stay outdoors, with the length of the work-out becoming a little longer!

MON	TUES	WED	THURS	FRI	SAT	SUN
OFF	Tennis with the girls	Go for a 30 minute Power-Walk	Go swimming for 30 minutes	OFF	Mind & Body Work-out	OFF
Video: Real Results 1 Work-out	OFF	Video: Rapid Results 2 Work-out	OFF	Real Results Complete Work-out	OFF	OFF
OFF	Tennis with the girls	Go for a 30 minute Power-Walk	Go swimming for 30 minutes	OFF	Mind & Body Work-out	OFF
Body Blasting Abdominal Work-out	OFF	Body Blasting Hips, Thighs, Buttocks Work-out	OFF	Body Blasting Chest, Back, Arm Work-out	OFF	OFF
OFF	Tennis with the girls	Go for a 30 minute Power-Walk	Go swimming for 30 minutes	OFF	Mind & Body Work-out	OFF

August

MON	TUES	WED	THURS	FRI	SAT	SUN
Video: Real Results 1 Work-out	OFF	Video: Rapid Results 2 Work-out	OFF	Real Results Complete Work-out	OFF	OFF
OFF	Tennis with the girls	Go for a 30 minute Power-Walk	Go swimming for 30 minutes	OFF	Cycling with the family	OFF
Summer Holidays	Body Blasting Abdominal Work-out	Body Blasting Hips, Thighs, Buttocks Work-out	Body Blasting Chest, Back, Arm Work-out	OFF	Mind & Body Work-out	OFF
Summer Holidays	Tennis with the family	Go for a 30 minute Power-Walk	Go swimming for 30 minutes	OFF	Cycling with the family	OFF
Video: Real Results 1 Work-out	OFF	Video: Rapid Results 2 Work-out	OFF	Real Results Complete Work-out	OFF	OFF

September

MON	TUES	WED	THURS	FRI	SAT	SUN
Take a week off - you've earned it!	Facial	Massage	Body Wrap	Manicure	OFF	OFF
OFF	Tennis with the girls	Go for a 30 minute Power-Walk	Go swimming for 30 minutes	OFF	Mind & Body Work-out	OFF
OFF	Body Blasting Abdominal Work-out	Body Blasting Hips, Thighs, Buttocks Work-out	Body Blasting Chest, Back, Arm Work-out	OFF	Cycling with the family	OFF
Video: Real Results 1 Work-out	OFF	Video: Rapid Results 2 Work-out	OFF	Real Results Complete Work-out	OFF	OFF
Body Blasting Abdominal Work-out	OFF	Body Blasting Hips, Thighs, Buttocks Work-out	OFF	Body Blasting Hips, Thighs, Buttocks Work-out	Go swimming with the family	OFF

October

With the weather getting cooler, and the temptation is there for big, hearty traditional meals, we'll have to put in a big effort in these last three months of the year. You now feel so great that you even want to tackle an aerobics class at the local leisure centre. Check out the instructor's qualifications, ask around and then make a decision as to which class you participate in.

MON	TUES	WED	THURS	FRI	SAT	SUN
Video: Real Results 1 Work-out	OFF	Video: Rapid Results 2 Work-out	OFF	Real Results Complete Work-out	OFF	OFF
OFF	Body Blasting Abdominal Work-out	Body Blasting Hips, Thighs, Buttocks Work-out	Body Blasting Chest, Back, Arm Work-out	OFF	Mind & Body Work-out	OFF
OFF	Aerobics with the girls	Mind & Body Work-out	Go swimming for 30 minutes	OFF	Cycling with the family	OFF
Video: Real Results 1 Work-out	Aerobics with the girls	Video: Rapid Results 2 Work-out	OFF	Real Results Complete Work-out	OFF	OFF
Body Blasting Abdominal Work-out	OFF	Body Blasting Hips, Thighs, Buttocks Work-out	OFF	Body Blasting Chest, Back, Arm Work-out	Mind & Body Work-out	OFF

November

MON	TUES	WED	THURS	FRI	SAT	SUN
Video: Real Results 1 Work-out	OFF	Video: Rapid Results 2 Work-out	OFF	Real Results Complete Work-out	OFF	OFF
OFF	Aerobics with the girls	Mind & Body Work-out	Aerobics with the girls	OFF	Swimming with the family	OFF
OFF	Body Blasting Abdominal Work-out	Body Blasting Hips, Thighs, Buttocks Work-out	Body Blasting Chest, Back, Arm Work-out	OFF	Mind & Body Work-out	OFF
OFF	Aerobics with the girls	Mind & Body Work-out	Aerobics with the girls	OFF	Swimming with the family	OFF
Video: Real Results 1 Work-out	OFF	Video: Rapid Results 2 Work-out	OFF	Real Results Complete Work-out	OFF	Mind & Body Work-out

December

MON	TUES	WED	THURS	FRI	SAT	SUN
OFF	Aerobics with the girls	Mind & Body Work-out	Aerobics with the girls	OFF	Swimming with the family	OFF
OFF	Body Blasting Abdominal Work-out	Body Blasting Hips, Thighs, Buttocks Work-out	Body Blasting Chest, Back, Arm Work-out	OFF	Mind & Body Work-out	OFF
Take a week off & get ready for Christmas	Facial	Massage	Body Wrap	Manicure	OFF	OFF
Video: Real Results 1 Work-out	Video: Rapid Results 2 Work-out	Real Results Complete Work-out	OFF	OFF	OFF	OFF
Body Blasting Abdominal Work-out	OFF	Body Blasting Hips, Thighs, Buttocks Work-out	OFF	Body Blasting Chest, Back, Arm Work-out	Mind & Body Work-out	OFF

Notes

Notes

Notes

Notes

Notes

Crucial Contacts

Amateur Swimming Association
Harold Fern House
Derby Square
Loughborough
Leicester
LE11 0AL
Tel: 01509 230431

Provides information on water polo, parent and baby activities, synchronised swimming, diving and much more. Gives details of local swimming clubs.

Aromatherapy Organisations Council
3 Latymer Close
Braybrooke
Market Harborough
Leicester
LE16 8LN
Tel: 01858 434242

Publishes a general information booklet listing schools and courses. Can provide details of qualified practitioners in your area.

British Association of Counselling
1 Regent Place
Rugby
Warwicks
CV21 2PJ
Tel: 01788 578328

Provides a national register of trained counsellors in your area. Also publishes a range of useful publications about counselling.

British Cycling Federation
National Cycling Centre
Stuart Street
Manchester
M11 4DQ
Tel: 0161 2302301

Provides information on local clubs for those interested in cycle sport.

British Massage Therapy Council
65a Adelphi Street
Preston
PR1 7BH
Tel: 01772 881063

Keeps details of courses in Swedish massage and sports massage. Can also provide details of local practitioners.

British Reflexology Association
Monks Orchard
Whitbourne
Worcester
WR6 5RB
Tel: 01886 821207

Provides a register of national members and details of courses.

The Eating Disorders Association
Sackville Place
44-48 Magdalen Street
Norwich
Norfolk
NR3 1JE

Send a stamped addressed envelope for help and advice in your area.

Exercise Association
Unit 4 Angel Gate
City Road
London
EC1V 2PT
Tel: 0171 2780811

The governing body for exercise and fitness. It promotes and monitors standards and provides information to the public and professionals.

Crucial Contacts (cont.)

Extend
22 Maltings Drive
Wheathampstead
Herts
AL4 8QT
Tel: 01582 832760

*Promotes exercise for men and women over 60.
Provides training courses for teachers and keeps a
register of those qualified to teach senior citizens.*

Health Education Authority
Hamilton House
Mableton Place
London
WC1H 9TX
Tel: 0171 3833833

*Promotes physical activity and health education.
Produces a range of publications for the public.*

Keep Fit Association
Francis House
Francis Street
London
SW1P 1DE
Tel: 0171 2338898

*Provides information on general exercise and
movement classes for all ages and abilities.*

Ramblers Association
1/5 Wandsworth Road
London
SW8 2XX
Tel: 0171 5826878

*Campaigns for access to moorland, woodland and
mountain area. The Association has 380 local
groups, and runs a year-round programme of walks.
Publishes useful information about walking.*

The Sports Council
16 Upper Woburn Place
London
WC1H 0QP
Tel: 0171 2731500

*Provides information and advice about sport,
including contacts of sports governing bodies and
organisations.*

Quitline 0800 002200

*A government-funded help line for those giving up
smoking. Provides information on smoking and local
support groups. Counsellors are on the end of the line
to support you through a difficult time. The service is
available 24 hours a day and is free.*